D1525528

EXPERIENCE
PUERTO RICO
LIKE A LOCAL

A Practical Pocket Guide For All Travelers

Caleb J. Smith

Map of Puerto Rico

Click here to View the Map of Puerto Rico (For e-book readers)

Scan the QR Code below with your mobile phone's Camera to View the Map of Puerto Rico (For Paperback Readers).

TABLE OF CONTENTS

INTRODUCTION

Puerto Rico, a vibrant Caribbean island, offers more than just sun and sand. It is a place rich in history, culture, and natural beauty. This guidebook is designed to take you on a journey through every corner of the island, from the bustling streets of San Juan to the quiet beauty of the central mountains. Whether you are a history buff, nature lover, or food enthusiast, Puerto Rico has something to surprise and delight you.

This book starts with the essentials: quick facts about the island, its history, and cultural insights that will deepen your appreciation and understanding of what you experience. We then prepare you for your visit, providing information on everything from visa requirements to packing tips. When you arrive, getting around is easy with our detailed guides to public transportation, car rentals, and more. We help you find the perfect place to stay, whether you're looking for luxury, a cozy hostel, or something in between.

Each region of Puerto Rico offers unique attractions and activities. In San Juan, explore historic forts and vibrant nightlife. In the east, find stunning rainforests and pristine beaches. The west is famous for its surf, and the south offers hidden gems off the usual tourist path. The central mountains provide a cool escape with lush coffee plantations.

Our guide does not just tell you where to go and what to see. We dive into the heart of Puerto Rican cuisine, exploring local specialties and where to find them. We also suggest shopping districts and items unique to the island that you might want to bring home. For those seeking adventure, we outline a variety of outdoor activities. Snorkel in crystal-clear waters, hike scenic trails, or play a round of golf with a view. We also spotlight cultural experiences, from music and dance to local festivals. Finally, we've included practical tips to help you travel smart and safe, along with comprehensive emergency information. Our appendices provide useful maps and resources to enrich your stay.

From the moment you start planning your trip to the time you return home, this guide aims to be an indispensable companion, ensuring that your visit to Puerto Rico is unforgettable. So, get ready to explore and be charmed by the island's incredible offerings. Let's start this exciting journey together!

CHAPTER 1

Understanding Puerto Rico

Puerto Rico is a land steeped in a rich tapestry of history and culture, colored by centuries of indigenous traditions and influences from Spain and Africa. This chapter aims to illuminate the multifaceted heritage that shapes the island today, guiding you through its historical evolution, cultural depth, and the vibrant celebrations that mark its calendar.

Our journey begins with a look back at the island's past, exploring significant events that have defined its course. From the early Taino inhabitants to Spanish colonization and its role in the New World, each period has left indelible marks on the island's identity. As we trace these historical threads, you'll gain insights into how Puerto Rico's modern character and spirit were forged. Moving beyond history, we delve into the island's cultural fabric. Here, you'll discover how everyday life pulses with a rhythm influenced by a blend of heritages. Music, art, and traditions are not just pastimes but are vital elements that express the soul of the Puerto Rican people. We'll explore how these cultural expressions continue to thrive, connecting the past with the present.

Finally, we highlight the festivals and events that fill the Puerto Rican calendar, offering a chance to experience its culture in its most exuberant forms. From lively street parades to solemn historical commemorations, these events are opportunities for visitors to immerse themselves in the joy and communal spirit of Puerto Rico. Each section of this chapter serves as a window into the heart of Puerto Rico, providing you with a deeper understanding of this enchanting island and enriching your visit. By the end of this chapter, you'll see Puerto Rico not just as a travel destination, but as a vibrant community with a story that continues to unfold.

Historical Overview

Puerto Rico's history is a compelling blend of struggle and transformation, which has played a pivotal role in the island's current identity. This detailed look at its past reveals how events have shaped the Puerto Rican way of life from ancient times to the present.

The story of Puerto Rico begins with the indigenous Taino people, who inhabited the island long before European arrival. They were skilled farmers and fishermen known for their elaborate ceremonies and crafts. The Tainos called the island 'Borikén,' which means "Land of the Valiant Lord."

In 1493, Christopher Columbus landed on the island during his second voyage to the New World, marking the beginning of Spanish influence. The Spaniards claimed the island, renaming it Puerto Rico, which means "Rich Port." This period introduced drastic changes as the Spanish settlers established towns and began cultivating crops like sugar cane, which would become a mainstay of the island's economy. The native Taino population, however, suffered greatly from diseases brought by Europeans and the harsh conditions of colonization.

Over the next few centuries, Puerto Rico became a crucial military outpost for Spain, with forts like El Morro and San Cristóbal built to protect against invasions. The island's strategic location in the Caribbean made it a target for other colonial powers. Despite these challenges, the people of Puerto Rico cultivated a distinct cultural identity, influenced by a mix of Spanish, African, and indigenous traditions.

The 19th century was marked by increasing pressure for autonomy from Spain. Movements and uprisings reflecting a desire for independence began to surface, most notably the Grito de Lares in 1868. Although this rebellion was not successful, it is celebrated today as a significant event in Puerto Rico's quest for recognition of its distinct identity.

In 1898, following the Spanish-American War, Puerto Rico was ceded to the United States as part of the Treaty of Paris. This transition brought about significant changes, including the establishment of a civilian government under the Foraker Act in 1900 and U.S. citizenship for Puerto Ricans in 1917. Throughout the 20th century, Puerto Rico underwent industrialization, especially during Operation Bootstrap in the mid-20th century, which aimed to transform its economy from agriculture-based to manufacturing-based.

Today, Puerto Rico is a modern place that retains its historical charm and cultural richness. Its colonial architecture, vibrant festivals, and the enduring spirit of its people tell the story of a land that has navigated colonization, cultural integration, and economic transformation. Understanding this history not only enriches a visit to the island but also deepens respect for the resilience and vitality of Puerto Ricans. The historical journey of Puerto Rico is a profound reminder of how the past and present blend to create the unique character of a place.

Cultural Insights

Puerto Rico, a melting pot of cultures, offers a rich tapestry of traditions and customs that make it a unique place to visit. This section dives deep into the cultural insights of Puerto Rico, exploring the elements that define its society and influence daily life on the island.

The cultural identity of Puerto Rico is primarily rooted in a blend of Spanish, African, and Taino (indigenous people) heritages. This mix is reflected in every aspect of Puerto Rican life, from its language to its culinary traditions, music, and religious practices. Spanish is the predominant language, but the influence of Taino and African dialects can be heard in the local expressions and slang that pepper everyday conversation. One of the most visible expressions of Puerto Rican culture is its music and dance, notably seen in genres like Salsa, Reggaeton, and Bomba. Salsa, which has spread worldwide, has deep roots on the island and is more than just music; it's a way of life, telling stories of love, heartbreak, and joy. Bomba, on the other hand, is a traditional dance and musical style that traces back to the island's African ancestry. It's a powerful display of resistance and celebration, where dancers lead the drummers in a dynamic, interactive performance.

Puerto Rican cuisine is another profound cultural element. It is a testament to the island's history, incorporating ingredients and cooking styles from its multi-ethnic heritage. Dishes like "mofongo" (mashed plantain with garlic, olive oil, and pork rinds), "arroz con gandules" (rice with pigeon peas), and "lechón asado" (roasted pork) showcase the island's culinary diversity. These meals are often shared during gatherings and festivities, highlighting the importance of food in social life and community bonding. Religious practices in Puerto Rico blend Catholic traditions with African and Taino beliefs, reflecting the island's historical layers. The majority of Puerto

Ricans are Roman Catholics, and religious festivals play a significant role in community life. One of the most significant events is the celebration of "Las Fiestas de la Calle San Sebastián" which marks the end of the Christmas season with a massive street festival featuring parades, music, and dancing.

Family plays a central role in Puerto Rican culture, with strong ties often extending beyond the immediate family to include a broad network of relatives. Family gatherings are frequent, spirited, and filled with music, food, and storytelling, serving as a key component of social life.

The art scene in Puerto Rico is vibrant, with numerous galleries, festivals, and an internationally recognized community of artists. Artistic expressions often explore themes of identity, colonialism, and resilience, offering insights into the island's past and its present.

Understanding these cultural aspects of Puerto Rico provides visitors with a deeper appreciation of the island's people and their heritage. It shows a society proud of its roots, yet dynamic and evolving. This rich cultural landscape invites travelers not just to observe but to participate and immerse themselves in a culture that is both ancient and refreshingly contemporary. Puerto Rico's culture is an integral part of its charm and a major reason why a visit to the island can be such a rewarding experience.

Festivals and Events Calendar

Puerto Rico is known for its dynamic festivals and events that showcase its rich culture and history throughout the year. These events are central to the island's way of life, providing vibrant displays of music, dance, food, and religious tradition. Exploring these celebrations gives visitors a deep insight into the heart and soul of Puerto Rican culture.

The festival calendar kicks off in January with the famous San Sebastián Street Festival in Old San Juan. This event marks the end of the Christmas season but feels like a party in its own right, with streets filled with music, crafts, food vendors, and parades. It draws both locals and tourists into a lively cultural celebration that lasts several days.

As the year progresses, the calendar features a variety of events that reflect Puerto Rico's diverse cultural makeup. One of the most significant is the Ponce Carnival, a pre-Lenten festival held in

February, similar to Mardi Gras. It features colorful parades, elaborate masks, and traditional "vejigante" costumes that blend Spanish, African, and Taino influences. The carnival is famous for its vibrant energy and the beauty of its traditions.

In March, the Casals Festival takes place, founded by famed cellist Pablo Casals. This classical music festival attracts musicians and audiences from around the world, celebrating classical and contemporary compositions in venues across San Juan.

Moving into summer, the Aibonito Flower Festival, held in late June to early July, transforms the mountain town of Aibonito into a floral paradise. This festival, the largest plant and flower show in Puerto Rico, includes exhibitions, sales, and a chance to enjoy the cooler mountain air.

August brings the Loíza Festival of Santiago Apostol, which is significant for its Afro-Puerto

Rican heritage. This event features traditional music, drumming, dance, and a variety of foods that celebrate the African legacy within Puerto Rican culture. The streets come alive with processions, traditional costumes, and masks, making it a profound cultural experience.

In the fall, the Puerto Rico Tip-Off welcomes basketball teams from various universities in the United States to compete in a tournament that attracts sports enthusiasts. This event not only highlights sports but also promotes interaction and enjoyment among locals and visitors.

As the year ends, Christmas is a major celebration, lasting from late November until January. The season is marked by "parrandas" or caroling processions, where groups of friends and family gather to sing traditional songs and enjoy festive foods like "pasteles" and "coquito," a coconut-based alcoholic beverage. Christmas in Puerto Rico is a unique blend of religious traditions and festive celebrations, culminating in large family gatherings and community joy.

Each of these festivals and events offers a window into the various aspects of Puerto Rican culture, from its music and culinary traditions to its religious practices and communal spirit. Participating in or observing these festivities can enrich a visitor's experience, providing not just fun but also a deeper understanding of the island's diverse cultural landscape.

CHAPTER 2

Before You Go

Planning your trip to Puerto Rico involves more than just booking flights and accommodations. To ensure a smooth and enjoyable visit, it's essential to prepare thoroughly before you set foot on the plane. This chapter covers all the critical steps to get ready for your Puerto Rican adventure, including understanding visa requirements, securing the right travel insurance, staying safe and healthy, and knowing what to pack.

First, we'll go over visa requirements. While U.S. citizens can travel freely to Puerto Rico as it's a U.S. territory, international visitors may need to check if they require a visa or follow specific entry protocols. Next, we emphasize the importance of travel insurance. Traveling with peace of mind knowing you are covered in case of unexpected medical issues or travel interruptions is crucial.

Health and safety tips are also key for any traveler. Puerto Rico is a safe destination, but like any travel experience, knowing local health advisories and safety guidelines can make your trip much smoother. We'll provide you with practical advice to avoid common health concerns and stay safe while exploring the island.

Finally, a packing list will help ensure you bring everything you need to enjoy Puerto Rico's diverse attractions, from its sunny beaches to its cool mountain regions. We'll guide you through selecting the right clothing, gadgets, and other essentials to make the most of your visit. By the end of this chapter, you'll be well-equipped with the knowledge and tips to ensure a hassle-free start to your journey, letting you focus on the excitement and beauty that await in Puerto Rico.

Visa Requirements

Understanding the visa requirements for visiting Puerto Rico is crucial for all travelers planning a trip to this vibrant island. Puerto Rico is a territory of the United States, so the visa requirements for entering Puerto Rico are the same as for any U.S. state. If you are a U.S. citizen, you do not need a passport or visa to enter Puerto Rico; a government-issued photo ID, such as a driver's license or ID card, is sufficient for travel.

For non-U.S. citizens, the requirements depend on your nationality and the reason for your visit. Most travelers from countries that participate in the Visa Waiver Program (VWP) can enter Puerto Rico without a visa for stays of 90 days or less. These travelers must obtain authorization through the Electronic System for Travel Authorization (ESTA) before their trip. It's important to handle this step online, well in advance of your travel dates, to avoid any last-minute issues.

Travelers from countries not included in the Visa Waiver Program will need to apply for a B-1 or B-2 visa, depending on the purpose of their visit. A B-1 visa is for those entering Puerto Rico for business-related reasons, while a B-2 visa is for tourists on vacation and those visiting for medical treatment or social events. The application process involves filling out forms, providing various documents, and attending an interview at a U.S. embassy or consulate in your home country.

It's also essential for all travelers to check the expiration date of their passport. The passport must be valid for the entire duration of your stay in Puerto Rico. Additionally, make sure you have proof of onward or return travel, as immigration officers might request it upon your arrival.

If you are planning a longer stay or considering moving to Puerto Rico for studies or work, you will need to apply for the appropriate visa that corresponds to your situation. Always check the latest information from official U.S. government websites or consult with an immigration lawyer to ensure you have the most accurate and up-to-date advice for your specific circumstances.

By understanding and complying with these visa requirements, you can ensure a smooth entry into Puerto Rico, letting you focus on enjoying the rich culture, beautiful landscapes, and warm hospitality that await you on the island.

Travel Insurance Essentials

Securing travel insurance is an essential step when planning your trip to Puerto Rico. Travel insurance provides peace of mind and financial protection against unexpected events, such as medical emergencies, trip cancellations, or lost luggage. Understanding the key elements of what should be included in your travel insurance for a trip to Puerto Rico can help ensure that you are well-prepared for any unforeseen circumstances.

Medical Coverage: Health care in Puerto Rico is of high quality but can be costly, especially for visitors who do not have local health insurance coverage. Your travel insurance should include comprehensive medical coverage that ensures you can receive medical attention without worrying about the expense. This should cover injuries, hospital stays, and possibly even medical evacuation if necessary. It's crucial to check that your insurance covers the costs of treating potentially serious diseases that might be contracted while traveling, such as dengue fever, which is present in the region.

Trip Cancellation: Trip cancellation insurance protects you in case you need to cancel your trip due to unforeseen events such as illness, a family emergency, or other eligible reasons. Ensure that the reasons for cancellation covered by your policy are extensive and review what documentation you would need to provide to make a claim.

Trip Interruption: Similar to cancellation insurance, trip interruption insurance covers you if you need to cut your trip short. This type of coverage is invaluable if you unexpectedly need to return home due to an emergency. The policy should cover additional travel expenses incurred to get you home quickly and safely.

Lost or Stolen Baggage: When traveling, there's always a risk of luggage being lost, delayed, or stolen. Insurance that covers the loss of personal items will help you replace the essentials and continue enjoying your trip without major inconveniences. This aspect of travel insurance typically covers clothing, toiletries, and other personal items. Some policies also cover high-value items like cameras and laptops, but there may be a cap on reimbursement for such items, so it's essential to understand the terms.

24-hour Assistance: Most travel insurance policies include a 24-hour helpline that you can call for assistance in an emergency, whether it's a medical issue, a lost passport, or travel disruptions. This service can be invaluable when you are in a different time zone or in need of assistance in a language you are not fluent in.

Natural Disasters and Weather-Related Coverage: Given that Puerto Rico is in a region that can experience hurricanes, consider a policy that includes coverage for natural disasters. This ensures that you can recover some of your costs if your travel plans are disrupted by severe weather.

Rental Car Coverage: If you plan to rent a car in Puerto Rico, check if your travel insurance includes rental car coverage. This can protect you in case of damage or theft of a rental vehicle and can be more cost-effective than buying insurance directly from the rental company.

When choosing a travel insurance policy, it's important to read the fine print and understand exactly what is and isn't covered. Look for exclusions and limits on claims, and consider paying a little extra for higher coverage limits if you feel it's necessary for your peace of mind. Choosing the right travel insurance allows you to explore Puerto Rico's beautiful landscapes and vibrant culture without worrying about the "what ifs," making your trip as relaxing and enjoyable as possible.

Health and Safety Tips

Visiting Puerto Rico is an exciting experience, but like any travel destination, it's important to consider health and safety tips to ensure a trouble-free trip. Here are some practical suggestions to keep in mind while exploring this beautiful island.

Firstly, health care in Puerto Rico is of a high standard, comparable to what you would expect in the mainland United States. Hospitals and clinics are well-equipped, and doctors are trained to a high standard, with many healthcare professionals fluent in English. However, it is advisable to have comprehensive travel insurance that covers medical expenses. This is because, while the healthcare is excellent, it can be expensive, especially for tourists who are not covered under local health plans.

Puerto Rico's tropical climate requires visitors to take certain health precautions. The sun can be very strong, so wearing high-factor sunscreen, sunglasses, and a hat is essential to protect against sunburn and heatstroke. Staying hydrated is also crucial, so carry water with you, especially when hiking or spending extended periods outside.

The island is home to various natural habitats, which means insects, particularly mosquitoes, are common. These mosquitoes can carry diseases such as Zika, Dengue, and Chikungunya. Using insect repellent and wearing long sleeves and pants during dawn and dusk when mosquitoes are most active can help prevent bites. It's also wise to stay in accommodations with air conditioning or screens on windows and doors to keep mosquitoes out.

Regarding safety, Puerto Rico is generally a safe destination for tourists. However, as in any tourist locale, petty crime like pickpocketing and theft can occur, especially in crowded areas such as popular tourist attractions and public transport hubs. To avoid becoming a target, keep your valuables secure and be aware of your surroundings. Avoid carrying large amounts of cash and consider using a money belt.

Driving in Puerto Rico can be challenging due to different traffic laws and road conditions. If you plan to rent a car, make sure you are familiar with local driving laws. Be particularly cautious when driving in the mountains or rural areas, where roads can be narrow and winding.

Natural disasters, such as hurricanes, can affect Puerto Rico, typically during the hurricane season from June to November. If you're visiting during these months, stay informed about the weather forecasts and understand the procedures for hurricane warnings. Most accommodations are well-prepared for such events and can provide guidance on what to do in case of a hurricane.

Lastly, Puerto Rico has strict laws regarding alcohol consumption. Drinking and driving are prohibited, and the legal drinking age is 18. Always consume alcohol responsibly and be aware of the local laws surrounding alcohol consumption in public places.

By following these health and safety tips, you can enjoy all that Puerto Rico has to offer without unnecessary risks, ensuring a memorable and safe experience on the island.

Packing List: Must-Have Items

When planning your trip to Puerto Rico, packing appropriately is key to ensuring you can fully enjoy everything the island has to offer, from its sunny beaches to its lush rainforests. Here's a comprehensive list of must-have items to include in your suitcase for a trip to this beautiful Caribbean destination.

Clothing: The weather in Puerto Rico is generally warm throughout the year, so lightweight and breathable clothing is a must. Pack plenty of t-shirts, shorts, and comfortable walking shoes for exploring during the day. Include a mix of casual and a few dressy options for evenings out. Since tropical showers can occur, especially if you're visiting between April and November, a lightweight rain jacket or a compact umbrella will be essential. Don't forget swimwear for the beach or poolside activities, along with a cover-up, which is handy for quick transitions from the beach to a casual restaurant.

Sun Protection: The Caribbean sun can be intense, so high SPF sunscreen is crucial to protect your skin from harmful UV rays. Reapply sunscreen every two hours, especially after swimming or sweating. A wide-brimmed hat and UV-protective sunglasses will also help shield you from the sun.

Insect Repellent: With Puerto Rico's tropical climate, mosquitoes are prevalent, especially in wetter areas and during the evening. An insect repellent will help protect you from mosquito bites that can transmit diseases like Zika and Dengue. Look for a repellent that contains DEET or Picaridin for effective protection.

Reusable Water Bottle: Staying hydrated is important in the tropical heat, and carrying a reusable water bottle will help you keep water on hand at all times. Many places offer water refills, making it easier to stay hydrated while reducing plastic usage.

Daypack: A comfortable, lightweight backpack is great for day trips and adventures around the island. It's perfect for carrying essentials like your water bottle, sunscreen, camera, and snacks while keeping your hands free.

Camera and Accessories: Puerto Rico's stunning landscapes, historic sites, and vibrant street scenes are incredibly photogenic. Bring a good camera to capture these moments. If you're planning on beach days or adventures like snorkeling, consider packing a waterproof phone case or an underwater camera.

Chargers and Adapters: Keep your electronic devices charged with the appropriate chargers. Although Puerto Rico uses the standard US plugs, it's always helpful to bring a portable power bank for those long days out when you might not have access to a power outlet.

Personal Medications and First Aid Kit: Pack any prescribed medications you need, along with a small first aid kit containing basics like band-aids, pain relievers, and antiseptic wipes. It's also wise to include remedies for common travel-related ailments such as upset stomach or motion sickness.

Copies of Important Documents: In case of emergency, it's important to have photocopies or digital copies of your important documents like your passport, ID, and insurance information. Keep these separate from the originals when you travel.

Snorkeling Gear: If you plan on exploring Puerto Rico's beautiful reefs and marine life, consider bringing your own snorkeling gear. While rentals are available, having your own ensures a perfect fit and comfort.

Packing these essentials will prepare you for a variety of activities and experiences in Puerto Rico, making your visit both enjoyable and comfortable. Remember, the key is to pack light and smart, bringing only what you need to make the most of your tropical getaway.

CHAPTER 3

Getting to and Around Puerto Rico

Navigating your way to and around Puerto Rico is an integral part of your travel adventure. This chapter provides a comprehensive guide on how to arrive and move around the island efficiently and enjoyably. Whether you are landing by plane, figuring out the best transportation options for your stay, or seeking tips to explore like a local, we have covered all the essentials to ensure a smooth experience.

Puerto Rico's main gateway is through its airports, with Luis Muñoz Marín International Airport in San Juan being the largest and most frequented. Understanding the layout of the airport, customs procedures, and transport options from the airport will help you commence your journey on the right foot. Besides air travel, we will discuss other points of entry and what to expect as you arrive.

Once on the island, getting around is an adventure in itself. Puerto Rico offers a range of transportation options suited for different tastes and budgets. Public buses, known as 'guaguas', are an economical way to travel, though they may be less reliable than what some travelers are accustomed to. For more flexibility, renting a car might be your best bet, and we will guide you through rental procedures, driving norms, and helpful tips to navigate the roads safely and confidently.

Additionally, for those looking to dive deeper into the local vibe, we offer insights into navigating the island as the locals do. From understanding the informal public transport vans, known as "públicos", to uncovering the shortcuts and favorite local spots, we provide tips that will help you move around the island with ease and authenticity. By the end of this chapter, you will be well-equipped with all the necessary information to travel within Puerto Rico confidently, allowing you to focus more on enjoying the stunning landscapes and vibrant culture that await you.

Arriving in Puerto Rico: Airports and Entry Points

Arriving in Puerto Rico is a straightforward process for most travelers, thanks to its status as a U.S. territory. The main entry point for international and mainland U.S. visitors is the Luis Muñoz Marín International Airport, located in Carolina, just outside the capital city of San Juan. This airport is the largest in Puerto Rico and serves as the hub for various international and domestic flights, connecting the island to multiple destinations worldwide.

Luis Muñoz Marín International Airport, often referred to by its airport code, SJU, handles over four million passengers annually. It features modern amenities, including a range of dining and shopping options, car rental agencies, and transportation services to help travelers continue their journey across the island. Upon landing, travelers will find the airport well-equipped to offer a smooth entry process, with clear signage and helpful staff to assist with immigration and customs procedures.

For those traveling from within the United States, entry into Puerto Rico is especially seamless, as there are no passport controls for U.S. citizens. However, it is advisable to carry some form of government-issued photo ID, such as a driver's license or passport. International visitors from other countries will need to adhere to the same entry requirements as they would when entering the United States, including possible visa requirements or ESTA approval for those from visa waiver countries.

In addition to the Luis Muñoz Marín International Airport, Puerto Rico can also be accessed through several smaller airports which handle mostly regional or charter flights. These include the Mercedita Airport in Ponce and the Rafael Hernández Airport in Aguadilla. Both airports provide additional options for travelers to reach different parts of the island directly.

Upon arrival, there are several ways to get from the airport to your final destination. Public transportation options such as buses and taxis are available, but many travelers find that renting a car provides the most flexibility for exploring the island. Car rental agencies are located at the airport, offering a range of vehicles to suit various preferences and budgets.

Alternatively, for those staying in San Juan or nearby areas, taxis and ride-sharing services are readily available at the airport. Fixed-rate fares are typically offered for taxis from the airport to major tourist zones in San Juan, making it easy to reach your accommodation without the hassle of negotiating prices.

For visitors looking to experience Puerto Rico like a local, public buses, known as "guaguas," provide an economical way to travel. However, it's important to note that while less expensive, buses might not offer the convenience and speed of taxis or rental cars, especially if you have significant luggage or are in a hurry.

By understanding these arrival procedures and transportation options, you can plan an efficient and stress-free start to your visit in Puerto Rico, ensuring more time to enjoy the island's attractions and beautiful scenery.

Transportation: From Public Buses to Car Rentals

Navigating through Puerto Rico offers various transportation options tailored to different preferences and needs, from public buses and taxis to car rentals. Understanding these choices will help you decide the best way to explore the island's beautiful landscapes and vibrant cities.

Public Buses: Puerto Rico has a public bus system, commonly referred to as "guaguas" by the locals. The buses in San Juan, the capital city, are operated by the Metropolitan Bus Authority (Autoridad Metropolitana de Autobuses, or AMA). The AMA offers extensive routes that cover much of the metropolitan area, including popular tourist destinations such as Old San Juan, Condado, and Isla Verde. Bus fares are economical, making this a budget-friendly option for getting around. However, it's important to note that while cost-effective, buses can be infrequent and may not always adhere to a strict schedule, which could be inconvenient for travelers on a tight timetable.

Taxis: Taxis are readily available throughout Puerto Rico, especially in major tourist areas and at the airport. They offer a more direct and faster means of transportation compared to buses. In San Juan, taxis operate with zone-based fares for trips to and from the airport and between major tourist zones. This makes it easy to know the cost upfront without the need for haggling. For travel outside these zones, taxis use meters, and it is advisable to confirm the fare with the driver before starting your journey.

Ride-Sharing Services: Ride-sharing services, such as Uber, are operational in Puerto Rico, mainly in the San Juan area. These services provide an alternative to traditional taxis and are often more economical. They can be especially convenient for visitors, as the fare and route are agreed upon digitally, eliminating potential language barriers and fare disputes.

Car Rentals: Renting a car provides the most flexibility and convenience for exploring Puerto Rico at your own pace. Car rental agencies are available at all major airports and in most larger towns and tourist areas. Having your own vehicle makes it easy to visit attractions that are difficult to reach via public transport, such as the El Yunque National Forest or remote beaches along the coast. Driving in Puerto Rico is similar to driving in the U.S., with road signs in Spanish and driving on the right-hand side of the road. However, travelers should be aware of local driving habits and occasionally challenging road conditions, especially in mountainous areas.

Ferries: For visits to islands like Vieques and Culebra, ferries are a practical transportation option. The main ferry terminal is located in Ceiba, on the east coast of Puerto Rico. Ferries run daily and offer an affordable way to access these popular islands, known for their stunning beaches and laid-back atmosphere.

When planning how to travel around Puerto Rico, consider what you want to see and do, as well as your budget and comfort level with different types of transportation. Each option has its own set of benefits, whether it's the affordability of public buses, the convenience of taxis and ride-sharing, or the independence provided by renting a car. By understanding the transportation landscape, you can make informed choices that enhance your visit, allowing you to experience all that Puerto Rico has to offer with ease and confidence.

Tips for Navigating Like a Local

Navigating Puerto Rico like a local involves more than just knowing your way around. It's about immersing yourself in the culture, understanding the local customs, and moving through the island with the ease of someone who belongs. Here are some invaluable tips that will help you explore Puerto Rico as if you were a seasoned local, enhancing your experience and perhaps even your speed and efficiency as you travel.

Learn Basic Spanish Phrases: While many Puerto Ricans are bilingual, speaking both Spanish and English, knowing some basic Spanish phrases will help you connect better with locals, especially in less touristy areas. Phrases like "¿Cuánto cuesta?" (How much does it cost?), "¿Dónde está...?" (Where is...?), and "Gracias" (Thank you) are not only polite but also practical.

Use Public Transportation Wisely: Locals know that while buses (guaguas) are economical, they aren't always reliable for strict schedules. For a truly local experience, try the públicos (public vans) that run specific routes and are often faster and more frequent than buses. They are a common way for locals to travel between cities and can be caught from major transport hubs.

Embrace the Island's Pace: Puerto Rico operates on 'island time,' which can be more relaxed than what some visitors may be used to. Embrace this slower pace and be flexible with your planning. Shops or offices may open a bit later than posted, and service at restaurants can be leisurely. Patience is not just a virtue here; it's a way of life.

Eat Where the Locals Eat: To truly eat like a local, venture beyond the main tourist spots. Look for roadside food stands or kiosks (kioskos) that offer local dishes such as alcapurrias, empanadillas, and lechón. These places often serve up the most authentic and delicious meals at prices significantly lower than in tourist-oriented restaurants.

Shop Local Markets: For fresh produce and unique local items, visit a mercado (market). Not only will you find fresh fruits, vegetables, and other local foods, but you'll also experience the lively atmosphere that is a staple of local life. Mercados are great places to practice your Spanish, sample local flavors, and pick up souvenirs that are locally produced.

Understand the Beach Culture: Beaches are central to life in Puerto Rico. Locals often go early in the morning or late in the afternoon to avoid the strongest sun. If you want to blend in, bring along a cooler with drinks and snacks, set up near other families and groups, and always clean up after yourself to respect the beautiful environment.

Respect the Local Customs: Puerto Ricans are generally very friendly and hospitable, but showing respect is important. Greet people with a smile, be polite, and dress appropriately, especially when visiting religious or culturally significant sites. Understanding and respecting local norms and customs will endear you to residents and enrich your experience.

By following these tips, you'll not only navigate Puerto Rico with the savvy of a local but also deepen your appreciation of the island's culture and people. This approach allows for a more authentic and memorable visit, filled with the warmth and vibrant spirit that Puerto Rico is known for.

CHAPTER 4

Accommodation Options

Finding the perfect place to stay is crucial for making your trip to Puerto Rico comfortable and memorable. Whether you're looking for the luxury of a high-end resort, the affordability of a hostel, or the unique charm of a local parador, Puerto Rico offers a diverse range of accommodations to suit every taste and budget. This chapter will guide you through the various options available, ensuring you find the ideal base for exploring the island's rich landscapes and vibrant culture.

Luxury seekers will be delighted with Puerto Rico's array of sophisticated resorts and boutique hotels, where exquisite service and top-notch facilities are designed to pamper guests. These establishments often boast prime locations with stunning ocean views, sprawling pools, and on-site dining of the highest quality.

For those traveling on a budget, there are numerous hostels and budget hotels that provide comfortable lodging without breaking the bank. These accommodations are ideal for travelers looking to prioritize experiences and adventure over luxury, offering clean, safe environments that cater to both solo travelers and families.

Lastly, for a truly unique experience, consider staying in one of Puerto Rico's paradores or eco-lodges. Paradores are locally owned properties that give guests a taste of traditional Puerto Rican hospitality and are often situated in scenic, rural areas, providing a peaceful retreat from the bustling city life. Eco-lodges offer a sustainable travel experience, perfect for nature lovers looking to minimize their environmental footprint while enjoying the natural beauty of the island. Each type of accommodation has its own set of benefits, and this chapter will help you navigate these options so you can select the best fit for your travel style and needs. By understanding what each category offers, you'll be well-equipped to make an informed decision, ensuring a comfortable stay that enhances your visit to Puerto Rico.

Luxury Resorts and Boutique Hotels

Luxury resorts and boutique hotels in Puerto Rico offer an exceptional level of comfort and exclusivity, appealing to those seeking a high-end vacation experience. These establishments are renowned for their personalized services, sophisticated decor, and prime locations that provide guests with unparalleled access to the island's most sought-after beaches and attractions.

Luxury resorts in Puerto Rico are typically located in scenic areas that maximize the natural beauty of their surroundings—whether that's a beachfront vista overlooking the Caribbean, a secluded spot near the lush rainforest of El Yunque, or the historic charm of Old San Juan. These resorts often feature expansive grounds with beautifully landscaped gardens, multiple swimming pools, spa facilities, fitness centers, and on-site gourmet restaurants offering exquisite dining experiences. Guests can expect spacious, elegantly furnished rooms with modern amenities that cater to every comfort.

The service at luxury resorts in Puerto Rico is aimed at providing a seamless and highly personalized experience. Many resorts offer concierge services to help guests plan and book activities, such as golf, water sports, and excursions around the island. Additional amenities often include room service, daily housekeeping, valet parking, and sometimes even butler service. For those traveling with families, many luxury resorts are equipped with children's clubs and activities that are creatively designed to entertain younger guests while providing relaxation for adults.

Boutique hotels in Puerto Rico, while smaller in scale compared to luxury resorts, do not spare any details in quality and charm. These hotels often reflect the unique character of their locales with locally inspired decor and architecture that integrates elements of Puerto Rican culture. Boutique hotels pride themselves on offering a more intimate and culturally rich experience. They often house fewer guests which allows for more personalized attention and an atmosphere that feels both upscale and homey.

Many boutique hotels are situated in renovated historic buildings that offer a glimpse into the island's past with modern luxury infused. They might not have the expansive list of amenities that larger resorts offer, but they make up for this with their unique style, exceptional service, and often more affordable pricing than larger resort counterparts.

Both luxury resorts and boutique hotels in Puerto Rico cater to those seeking an exceptional stay where they can relax in comfort, enjoy the local culture, and experience the best that Puerto Rican hospitality has to offer. Whether you are honeymooning, celebrating an anniversary, or simply in need of a luxurious escape, these accommodations provide an ideal setting for a memorable vacation.

In addition, here are some top recommendations for luxury resorts and boutique hotels. Each of these venues is renowned for its exceptional service, beautiful surroundings, and premium amenities.

1. The St. Regis Bahia Beach Resort

- **Location:** State Road 187 kilometer 4.2, Rio Grande 00745, Puerto Rico
- **Phone:** +1 787-809-8000
- **Email:**reservations.bahiabeach@stregis.com
- **Website:**(https://www.marriott.com/hotels/travel/sjuxr-the-st-regis-bahia-beach-resort-puerto-rico/)
- **Price Range:** $700 - $1500 per night
- **Amenities:** This resort offers a private beach, a golf course, a spa, and several

dining options. Each guest room features luxurious furnishings and modern amenities.

- **Getting There:** The resort is approximately a 30-minute drive from Luis Muñoz Marín International Airport. Guests can arrange for a private transfer, rent a car, or take a taxi.

2. Dorado Beach, A Ritz-Carlton Reserve

- **Location:** 100 Dorado Beach Drive, Dorado 00646, Puerto Rico
- **Phone:** +1 787-626-1100
- **Email:** Contact via website
- **Website:**(https://www.ritzcarlton.com/en/ hotels/puerto-rico/dorado-beach)
- **Price Range:** $1,000 - $4,500 per night
- **Amenities:** Features include direct beach access, a championship golf course, a luxurious spa, and fine dining establishments. The resort offers a

personalized and private experience in a stunning natural setting.

- **Getting There:** Located about 40 minutes west of San Juan by car. Guests can opt for a taxi, a private car service, or a rental car from the airport.

3. Condado Vanderbilt Hotel

- **Location:** 1055 Ashford Avenue, San Juan 00907, Puerto Rico
- **Phone:** +1 787-721-5500
- **Email:**reservations@condadovanderbilt.com
- **Website:**(https://www.condadovanderbilt.com)
- **Price Range:** $300 - $1,000 per night
- **Amenities:** Historic hotel with luxurious rooms, ocean views, an infinity pool, multiple dining options, and a renowned spa.
- **Getting There:** This hotel is conveniently located in the popular Condado area of

San Juan, just 10 minutes from Luis Muñoz Marín International Airport. Airport transfers, taxis, and rental cars are readily available.

4. Hotel El Convento

- **Location:** 100 Calle del Cristo, San Juan 00901, Puerto Rico
- **Phone:** +1 787-723-9020
- **Email:** reservations@elconvento.com
- **Website:** (https://www.elconvento.com)
- **Price Range:** $200 - $500 per night
- **Amenities:** A historic boutique hotel in the heart of Old San Juan, featuring elegant accommodations, a plunge pool, and a rooftop terrace offering spectacular views of the city.
- **Getting There:** Located in the historic Old San Juan district, about 15 minutes by car from the airport. The area is also accessible via taxi or a pre-arranged airport shuttle.

These hotels offer a blend of luxury, comfort, and distinctive local flavor, making them perfect choices for those looking to indulge while exploring the beauty and culture of Puerto Rico.

Budget Stays and Hostels

For those looking to explore Puerto Rico without breaking the bank, budget stays and hostels offer affordable and comfortable accommodations. These options are perfect for travelers who prioritize experiences and adventures over luxury, providing a cost-effective way to enjoy the beauty and culture of the island.

Budget accommodations in Puerto Rico vary widely, from cozy guesthouses to lively hostels that cater to backpackers, solo travelers, and families alike. These establishments are typically found throughout the island, including both major cities like San Juan and quieter, more rural areas. They offer a unique opportunity not only to save money but also to meet other travelers and locals, providing a richer travel experience.

Hostels in Puerto Rico often feature dormitory-style rooms with shared bathrooms, though many also offer private rooms for those seeking a bit more privacy. Common areas, like lounges and kitchens, encourage a communal atmosphere where guests can cook meals, share travel tips, and organize group outings. This can be particularly appealing to solo travelers looking to connect with others during their journey.

Many budget stays and hostels also provide amenities tailored to the needs of budget-conscious travelers, including free Wi-Fi, breakfast, and laundry facilities. Some may offer additional perks like bicycle rentals, which are a great way to explore nearby attractions without the cost of car rentals or taxis.

Additionally, the locations of these accommodations often provide easy access to public transportation routes, making it convenient to explore major sights without the need for a car. For example, hostels in the Old San Juan area allow travelers to walk to nearby museums, historic sites, and vibrant nightlife, while those outside the city may offer closer proximity to natural attractions like beaches or hiking trails.

Budget accommodations are not only about saving money; they also offer a closer look at local life. Many are run by locals who are eager to share their knowledge of the area, offering insights that aren't typically available in larger hotels. They might recommend lesser-known restaurants, hidden gems, and special events known only to residents, enhancing your experience of Puerto Rican culture and hospitality.

For travelers on a tight budget, or for those who simply prefer a more laid-back and social lodging option, Puerto Rico's hostels and budget accommodations provide an excellent base for exploring the island. These stays balance cost, comfort, and convenience, allowing you to invest more in your adventures across Puerto Rico.

In addition, here are some highly recommended hostels and budget accommodations. These options not only offer affordability but also provide comfortable lodging and a friendly atmosphere.

1. Island Time Hostel

- **Location:** 1050 Calle Mariana, San Juan, 00907, Puerto Rico
- **Phone:** +1 787-998-5466
- **Email:** islandtimehostel@gmail.com
- **Website:**(http://www.islandtimehostel.com)
- **Price Range:** $20 - $50 per night
- **Amenities:** This hostel offers both dormitory beds and private rooms, with a shared kitchen, free Wi-Fi, and a lounge area. It's known for its friendly staff and clean facilities.
- **Getting There:** Located in the vibrant area of Santurce in San Juan, it's easily accessible by taxi or bus from Luis Muñoz

Marín International Airport, approximately 10 kilometers away.

2. San Juan International Hostel

- **Location:** 1452 Calle América, San Juan, 00909, Puerto Rico
- **Phone:** +1 787-728-3661
- **Website:**(https://www.hostelworld.com/ho steldetails.php/San-Juan-International-Hos tel/San-Juan/278498)
- **Price Range:** $15 - $40 per night
- **Amenities:** This hostel features dorm-style rooms with air conditioning, a communal kitchen, luggage storage, and free Wi-Fi. It's popular among backpackers for its affordable rates and central location.
- **Getting There:** Situated in the central part of San Juan, it is accessible via bus or taxi from the airport. The hostel is close to local bus lines that provide access to major attractions.

3. MoonLight Bay Hostel

- **Location:** 478 Calle Luna, Fajardo, 00740, Puerto Rico
- **Phone:** +1 787-801-2871
- **Email:**moonlightbayhostel@gmail.com
- **Website:**(http://www.moonlightbayhostel.com)
- **Price Range:** $30 - $80 per night
- **Amenities:** Located near the Fajardo ferry terminal, this hostel offers private and dorm rooms, a rooftop terrace, and a kitchen. It's a favorite for those heading to the nearby islands of Vieques and Culebra.
- **Getting There:** Fajardo is about 60 kilometers east of San Juan. The hostel is easily accessible by car or public transport from the capital, with clear signage and local buses stopping nearby.

4. Casa Santurce

- **Location:**105 Calle del Parque, San Juan, 00911, Puerto Rico

- **Phone:** +1 787-538-6724
- **Email:** info@casasanturce.com
- **Website:** (https://www.casasanturce.com)
- **Price Range:** $25 - $60 per night
- **Amenities:** Nestled in the heart of Santurce, this charming hostel offers an outdoor terrace, a communal lounge, and kitchen facilities. It's perfect for travelers looking for a cozy, home-like atmosphere.
- **Getting There:** The hostel is centrally located and just a short bus ride or taxi drive from the airport, near popular attractions and local dining spots.

These budget stays and hostels are excellent choices for travelers who wish to explore Puerto Rico without overspending on accommodations. Each offers unique perks and is located in areas with good transport links, making them convenient bases for touring the island.

Unique Accommodations: Paradores and Eco-Lodges

In Puerto Rico, travelers seeking a distinctive and immersive lodging experience can choose from a range of unique accommodations such as paradores and eco-lodges. These establishments are renowned for offering more than just a place to stay—they provide a deeper connection to the local culture and environment.

Paradores of Puerto Rico are a network of family-owned accommodations that are situated in culturally and historically significant areas. These small hotels are often located in renovated historic buildings or in picturesque rural settings that offer easy access to beautiful landscapes and local activities. Paradores are endorsed by the Puerto Rican Tourism Company, ensuring they meet specific standards of hospitality and authenticity. Guests at paradores can expect personalized service, local cuisine, and an ambiance that reflects the heritage of the area. Staying at a parador is ideal for travelers who wish to experience Puerto Rico's history and regional traditions up close.

Eco-Lodges in Puerto Rico provide an eco-friendly approach to hospitality, placing a strong emphasis on sustainability and minimal environmental impact. These lodges are typically set in remote, natural locations that allow guests to unwind in tranquility while being surrounded by nature. Eco-lodges are built using sustainable materials and practices, often incorporating renewable energy sources, water conservation measures, and waste reduction programs. They offer a range of nature-based activities such as bird watching, hiking, and guided environmental tours. The accommodations are designed to blend into the landscape, offering comfort without the excesses of traditional tourist resorts.

Eco-lodges are particularly popular among nature enthusiasts, conservationists, and those who wish to have a low-carbon footprint during their travels. By staying in an eco-lodge, visitors not only enjoy the natural beauty of Puerto Rico but also contribute to the conservation efforts that protect these environments for future generations.

Both paradores and eco-lodges in Puerto Rico cater to travelers looking for a meaningful and enriching travel experience. They provide opportunities to learn about the local ecosystem, participate in conservation efforts, and immerse oneself in the cultural narrative of the island. Whether it's the charm of a parador or the rustic appeal of an eco-lodge, these unique accommodations are perfect for those who seek a deeper connection with their destination.

In addition, here are recommended paradores and eco-lodges across the island. Each offers a distinctive stay with a commitment to cultural heritage and environmental sustainability.

1. Parador Guánica 1929

- **Location:** Road 3116, Km 2.5, Guánica, Puerto Rico, 00653
- **Phone:** +1 787-821-0099
- **Email:** info@paradorguanica.com
- **Website:**(https://www.paradorguanica.com)
- **Price Range:** $95 - $150 per night
- **Amenities:** This historic hotel offers a swimming pool, access to nearby beaches, and a restaurant serving local cuisine. It is situated in a tranquil area, ideal for relaxation and nature walks.
- **Getting There:** Located in the small town of Guánica, it is about a 2-hour drive from San Juan. The journey can be made by car via PR-52 and PR-116.

2. Parador Villa Parguera

- **Location:** Calle 304, La Parguera, Lajas, Puerto Rico, 00667
- **Phone:** +1 787-899-7777
- **Email:** info@villaparguera.com
- **Website:** (http://www.villaparguera.com)
- **Price Range:** $120 - $180 per night
- **Amenities:** Features include picturesque views of the Caribbean, an outdoor pool, and boat trips to the bioluminescent bay. The parador is known for its peaceful setting and water-based activities.
- **Getting There:** Villa Parguera is located in the southwest of the island, accessible from San Juan by a 2.5-hour drive on PR-2 and PR-116.

3. Casa Grande Mountain Retreat

- **Location:** Road 612, Km 0.3, Utuado, Puerto Rico, 00641
- **Phone:** +1 787-894-3939
- **Email:** info@hotelcasagrande.com

- **Website:**(https://www.hotelcasagrande.com)
- **Price Range:** $100 - $150 per night
- **Amenities:** Set in the mountains of Utuado, this eco-lodge offers yoga retreats, an outdoor pool, and a café serving vegetarian cuisine. It's a favorite for those seeking a retreat from the hustle and bustle of city life.
- **Getting There:** Approximately 1.5 hours from San Juan, accessible via PR-22 and PR-111. The scenic drive highlights the lush interior of the island.

4. Hix Island House

- **Location:** Route 995, Km. 1.5, Vieques, Puerto Rico, 00765
- **Phone:** +1 787-741-2302
- **Email:** reservations@hixislandhouse.com
- **Website:**(https://www.hixislandhouse.com)
- **Price Range:** $150 - $300 per night

- **Amenities:** An eco-lodge offering modern lofts within a 13-acre natural preserve on Vieques Island. Solar power, rainwater harvesting, and eco-friendly practices are part of the stay experience. It's an ideal choice for eco-conscious travelers.
- **Getting There:** Vieques can be reached by a short flight from San Juan or by ferry from Ceiba. Hix Island House is a short drive from both the Vieques airport and ferry terminal.

These unique accommodations in Puerto Rico provide more than just a place to sleep; they offer a gateway to exploring the island's rich cultural heritage and pristine natural environments. Whether nestled in a historic town or perched in the lush mountains, each place promises a memorable and enriching experience.

CHAPTER 5

Eating and Drinking in Puerto Rico

Puerto Rico offers a rich tapestry of culinary experiences that reflect its cultural diversity, from traditional dishes that tell the story of the island's history to contemporary dining that showcases modern culinary innovations. This chapter will guide you through a gastronomic journey across Puerto Rico, featuring everything from casual street food vendors to upscale restaurants, as well as vibrant nightlife spots where food, drink, and music create a lively evening ambiance.

Embarking on culinary tours is an excellent way to dive into Puerto Rico's food scene. These tours help visitors explore a variety of local flavors in settings that range from bustling street markets to gourmet kitchens. You'll learn about the island's staple ingredients, traditional cooking methods, and innovative culinary techniques that make Puerto Rican cuisine stand out in the Caribbean.

The island's local specialties are a reflection of its rich cultural mix, incorporating influences from Spanish, African, and Taino cuisines. Dishes like mofongo, made from mashed plantains with garlic and pork, and lechón, a slow-roasted marinated pork, are not just meals but a feast for the senses. This chapter will point you to the best places to sample these dishes and more, ensuring you know exactly where to go to satisfy your culinary curiosities.

As the sun sets, Puerto Rico's nightlife comes alive with an array of options to suit any mood. From laid-back beach bars where you can sip a piña colada under the stars to vibrant clubs and live music venues in San Juan, the island offers plenty of opportunities to enjoy local rum and dance to both traditional salsa and modern reggaeton.

In this chapter, we will uncover the best spots for eating, drinking, and experiencing the dynamic social scene of Puerto Rico, making sure you fully enjoy the island's festive spirit and delectable flavors. Whether you're a foodie looking for the next great meal or someone who enjoys the occasional night out, you'll find plenty of options to make your visit to Puerto Rico deliciously unforgettable.

Culinary Tours: From Street Food to Fine Dining

Exploring Puerto Rico through its food is an adventure that can take you from bustling street corners with vibrant food vendors to elegant dining rooms in top-tier restaurants. Culinary tours across the island offer a diverse palette of flavors that embody the cultural fusion at the heart of Puerto Rican cuisine. These tours provide an invaluable insight into both the history and modern evolution of local dishes, making them a must-do activity for any food enthusiast visiting the island.

Street Food Delights

One of the best ways to dive into Puerto Rican cuisine is to start with its street food. Across the island, particularly in major cities like San Juan, Ponce, and Mayagüez, you'll find an array of street vendors and food trucks serving up local favorites. Delicacies such as "alcapurrias" (stuffed fritters), "bacalaítos" (salt cod fritters), and "pinchos" (skewered meats), offer quick, delicious tastes of traditional flavors. San Juan's La Placita de Santurce transforms into a lively outdoor market by day and a popular street food haven by night, where locals and tourists mingle over shared meals.

Fine Dining and Gourmet Experiences

For a more refined culinary experience, Puerto Rico boasts several high-end restaurants that blend local ingredients with international cooking techniques. In the Condado and Old San Juan districts, establishments like "Marmalade" and "1919 Restaurant" stand out for their innovative menus created by renowned chefs. These restaurants often feature tasting menus that take diners on a gastronomic journey through multiple courses paired with exquisite wines.

Culinary Tours and Cooking Classes

Various organized tours are available for those who wish to have a structured exploration of

Puerto Rico's culinary landscape. These tours can range from guided walks through historic neighborhoods with stops at notable eateries to cooking classes where participants learn to make traditional Puerto Rican dishes under the guidance of local chefs. For instance, "Spoons Food Tours" and "Flavors of San Juan" provide immersive experiences that combine cultural insights with culinary delights, allowing visitors to learn about the island's food heritage while tasting it firsthand.

Getting There

Most culinary tours and experiences are centered in and around San Juan, given its status as the capital and largest city. Travelers can easily access these tours by staying in San Juan or by driving in from other parts of the island—San Juan is reachable via major highways like PR-52 and PR-22 from southern and western Puerto Rico, respectively. Public transportation and taxis are also available for those who prefer not to drive.

By joining a culinary tour in Puerto Rico, visitors not only treat their taste buds to extraordinary flavors but also gain a deeper understanding of the island's cultural fabric, woven through its cuisine. Whether it's the rustic charm of street foods or the sophisticated ambiance of fine dining, Puerto Rico offers a culinary adventure that is as diverse as it is delicious.

Local Specialties and Where to Find Them

Puerto Rico's culinary landscape is a vibrant tapestry woven from the island's rich history, cultural diversity, and abundant natural resources. This has given birth to an array of local specialties that are as varied as they are delicious. Here, we delve into some of these unique dishes and suggest where to find them to ensure a truly authentic Puerto Rican dining experience.

Mofongo is arguably one of the most iconic Puerto Rican dishes. Made from mashed green plantains mixed with garlic, olive oil, and pork cracklings, it is often filled with chicken, shrimp, or steak and served with a flavorful broth. For some of the best mofongo, visit Café El Punto in Old San Juan, where the dish is prepared to perfection with a choice of enticing fillings and sauces.

Lechón, or roasted pork, is another staple of Puerto Rican cuisine, particularly celebrated in the town of Guavate, located in the central mountainous region of the island. Here, the route known as "Ruta del Lechón" features a string of lechoneras (roast pork eateries) such as El Rancho Original, where the pork is slow-roasted over open flames, resulting in succulent meat with crispy, flavorful skin.

Arroz con gandules (rice with pigeon peas) is the quintessential Puerto Rican side dish, combining rice, pigeon peas, pork, olives, capers, and a blend of spices cooked together for a hearty and aromatic dish. This dish is commonly found at local festivals and casual diners, but for an elevated version, visit La Casita Blanca in Santurce, where it is often served as part of a traditional Puerto Rican meal.

Pastelillos de carne (meat turnovers) are fried or baked pastries filled with seasoned meat, chicken, or seafood. These can be found in many local bakeries and street vendors, but for something special, head to Kiosko El Boricua in Luquillo, where the pastelillos are known for their flaky pastry and rich fillings.

Alcapurrias are another popular street food item, consisting of fritters made from a dough of grated yuca (cassava) or green bananas, filled with ground beef, chicken, or crab, then deep-fried to crispy perfection. They are a staple at beach kiosks along Piñones, a coastal stretch where Kiosko La Comay offers some of the best examples, served hot and crispy from the fryer.

Desserts like flan (a caramel custard) and tembleque (a coconut pudding) round off any Puerto Rican meal on a sweet note. Dulces de Lares in the town of Lares is a renowned bakery that offers an array of traditional sweets, including excellent versions of both desserts.

Each of these dishes represents a story of Puerto Rican culture and tradition, and finding them in their ideal settings—whether a bustling city café or a roadside stall in the countryside—adds an enriching layer to the dining experience. Through these foods, visitors not only satiate their hunger but also gain insights into the heart of Puerto Rican life and its culinary heritage.

Nightlife: Bars, Clubs, and Live Music Venues

Puerto Rico's nightlife offers an exhilarating mix of bars, clubs, and live music venues that reflect the island's vibrant culture and love for celebration. Whether you're in the mood for sipping artisan cocktails, dancing to the beat of reggaeton, or enjoying live salsa music, the island has something to cater to every taste.

San Juan, the capital, is the heart of Puerto Rico's nightlife and offers a variety of experiences. The district of Condado is known for its upscale bars and lounges where mixologists serve creative cocktails using local ingredients. Here, places like La Factoría in Old San Juan, a multi-level bar known for its innovative drinks and lively salsa nights, are a must-visit. This venue has garnered international fame and perfectly encapsulates the cocktail culture of Puerto Rico. To get there, visitors staying in Condado or Old San Juan can easily take a short taxi ride or even enjoy a scenic walk through the historic streets.

For those interested in a clubbing experience, La Placita de Santurce transforms from a traditional market square by day into a bustling nightlife hub by night. Clubs and bars in this area often feature live DJs and themed party nights, attracting a diverse crowd looking to dance the night away. The vibrant atmosphere here is representative of the island's party spirit, and it's easily accessible via taxi or bus from most parts of San Juan.

For live music enthusiasts, Santurce is also home to venues like El Boricua, which offers an authentic Puerto Rican experience with local bands playing genres ranging from salsa and bomba to reggaeton and bachata. This spot is particularly popular on weekends and provides a deep dive into the local music scene. It's located just a short drive from downtown San Juan, and public transport options are readily available.

Heading outside the capital, the town of Ponce in the south also boasts a lively nightlife scene with a more laid-back vibe. Here, venues like La Guarida del Blues offer live blues and rock performances in a cozy setting, ideal for music lovers looking for a night out with a different flavor. Ponce is accessible by car from San Juan via the PR-52 highway, a journey that takes about an hour and a half, making it an easy getaway for an evening.

In addition to bars and clubs, Puerto Rico hosts numerous festivals and events throughout the year that feature night markets, live music, and cultural performances, particularly during holiday periods. These events are spread across the island and offer visitors a chance to see how nightlife blends with local traditions and celebrations.

No matter where you find yourself in Puerto Rico, the key to enjoying the nightlife is to embrace the local way of celebrating life. Each venue and each district offers its own unique flavor and experience, reflecting the rich cultural tapestry of this vibrant Caribbean island. Whether you're walking down the cobbled streets of Old San Juan to a hidden bar or dancing under the stars in La Placita, Puerto Rico's nightlife is sure to provide unforgettable memories.

CHAPTER 6

Shopping and Souvenirs

Shopping in Puerto Rico offers a delightful array of opportunities, from modern malls filled with international brands to local artisan markets that showcase the island's rich cultural heritage. This chapter will explore the diverse shopping districts where you can find everything from the latest fashion trends to unique, handmade crafts that embody the spirit of the island.

As you stroll through Puerto Rico's shopping landscapes, you'll encounter bustling markets that are a feast for the senses. Here, local artisans sell their wares, ranging from intricately carved santos (hand-carved religious figures) and vibrant vejigante masks to handwoven textiles and finely crafted jewelry. These markets not only provide a chance to pick up unique souvenirs but also to interact with the artisans themselves, gaining insights into the traditions and techniques behind their creations.

In addition to these artisan treasures, Puerto Rico's shopping districts include well-appointed malls and boutique stores that offer a variety of goods, from luxury items to popular retail brands. Whether you're in San Juan's Plaza Las Américas, the Caribbean's largest shopping mall, or the charming boutiques of Old San Juan, you'll find plenty of options to satisfy your shopping desires.

This chapter will guide you through the best places to hunt for souvenirs and gifts that will serve as mementos of your Puerto Rican adventure. From the cobblestone streets lined with local shops to the gleaming corridors of expansive shopping centers, you'll discover the perfect items to bring home. Each shopping destination provides a unique glimpse into the island's blend of old and new, ensuring that your shopping experiences are as enriching as they are enjoyable.

Shopping Districts: From Artisan Markets to Malls

Puerto Rico's shopping districts offer a fascinating blend of options, ranging from vibrant artisan markets to expansive, modern malls. Each shopping venue provides visitors with unique insights into the island's culture and lifestyle, as well as opportunities to purchase everything from everyday items to unique souvenirs that are deeply rooted in Puerto Rican heritage.

Artisan Markets

Artisan markets are a key feature of Puerto Rico's shopping scene, particularly noted for their celebration of local crafts and traditions. These markets are ideal for finding handcrafted goods such as traditional santos (wooden saints), colorful vejigante masks used during festivals, and handmade lace known as mundillo. One of the most famous markets is the San Juan Artisan Market, held weekly in Old San Juan. Here, artisans display their crafts along the picturesque walkways of Plaza San José and Plaza del Mercado. This market is easily accessible by foot within the historic district, and visitors staying in other parts of San Juan can reach it by bus, taxi, or a short car ride.

Street Vendors

Alongside the more organized markets, street vendors can be found across various parts of the island, particularly in tourist-heavy areas such as Condado and Isla Verde. These vendors often sell arts and crafts, jewelry, and small souvenirs that are perfect for gifts. Strolling through these areas offers a more casual shopping experience and the opportunity to engage directly with the local community.

Shopping Malls

For a more traditional shopping experience, Puerto Rico offers several large shopping malls that feature a mix of local and international brands. Plaza Las Américas in San Juan, the largest shopping mall in the Caribbean, houses over 300 stores along with numerous restaurants and cinemas. Located centrally in the Hato Rey district of San Juan, it is accessible via major highways like PR-18 and PR-22, making it a convenient option for both locals and tourists. Parking is ample, and public transit routes service the mall as well, making it easy to visit without personal transportation.

Luxury Shopping

For high-end shopping, The Mall of San Juan offers luxury brands and boutiques. This relatively new shopping center is located near the San Juan airport, making it an easy stop for travelers. It features upscale retailers as well as dining options that cater to a more refined palate. The mall is accessible via PR-26, and there is significant taxi and bus service due to its proximity to the airport and major hotels.

These shopping venues not only offer goods but also an experience that is deeply intertwined with the culture and lifestyle of Puerto Rico. Whether you're browsing through handcrafted art at a bustling market or perusing high-end boutiques in a state-of-the-art mall, the island's shopping districts provide a rich tapestry of choices that cater to every taste and budget. This diversity ensures that every visitor can find something special to take home, from affordable crafts to luxury goods, embodying the vibrant spirit and heritage of Puerto Rico.

Puerto Rican Crafts and Souvenirs to Bring Home

Bringing home a piece of Puerto Rico is a cherished tradition for many travelers, and the island offers an array of distinctive crafts and souvenirs that reflect its rich cultural heritage. These items not only serve as mementos but also help support local artisans and preserve the traditional crafts that are a fundamental part of Puerto Rican culture.

Santos - One of the most iconic Puerto Rican crafts is the santo. These hand-carved wooden figures represent saints and are part of a long-standing religious and cultural tradition. Santos are typically carved from tropical hardwoods and are either painted or left in their natural wood finish. Each piece is unique, often passed down through generations, and is considered a collector's item. Artisans who create these figures are known as santeros, and their work can be found in specialty shops and local markets, particularly in the towns of San Juan and Ponce.

Vejigante Masks - Another distinctive craft is the vejigante mask, used during various festivals, especially the Ponce Carnival and Loiza's St. James Festival. These colorful masks, made from coconut shells, papier-mâché, or fiberglass, are painted in bright colors and adorned with horns. Vejigante masks represent a folkloric figure that blends Spanish, African, and Taino traditions. They are not only a popular souvenir but also a piece of Puerto Rican festive culture.

Mundillo Lace - For those who appreciate delicate crafts, mundillo (bobbin lace) is a fine choice. This intricate lace-making technique was brought to the island in the 16th century and continues to thrive in the town of Moca, where there are shops and small factories dedicated to mundillo. Items such as doilies, table runners, and clothing featuring this lace are exquisite gifts that showcase the meticulous craftsmanship of Puerto Rican artisans.

Puerto Rican Rum - Beyond crafts, Puerto Rico is famous for its rum, which is considered among the best in the world. Distilleries across the island offer tours and tastings, and bottles of rum can be purchased as souvenirs. Premium brands like Don Q, Ron del Barrilito, and Bacardi have special editions that are perfect for taking home.

Coffee - Puerto Rican coffee is renowned for its rich flavor and high quality, cultivated in the island's central mountains. Coffee plantations offer tours that provide insights into the coffee-making process from bean to cup. Bags of locally grown coffee are a popular souvenir and a way of remembering the island's aromatic flavors.

These crafts and products are available in various locations across the island. For a comprehensive experience, Old San Juan offers numerous shops where these items are sold, providing authenticity certificates for crafts like santos and mundillo. Additionally, local markets such as the Santurce Market or the Ponce Market are excellent places to find these items, offering the added benefit of interacting directly with the artisans.

When purchasing these souvenirs, not only are you bringing home a piece of Puerto Rican heritage, but you are also supporting the local economy and helping to keep traditional crafts alive. Each item tells a story of the island's history, culture, and people, making it a meaningful reminder of your visit to Puerto Rico.

CHAPTER 7

Exploring Puerto Rico: Region by Region

Puerto Rico, a vibrant island rich in culture, history, and natural beauty, offers diverse experiences across its various regions. Each area presents its unique attractions, from the historical depths of its capital to the serene beauty of its remote beaches and mountains. This chapter will guide you through a detailed exploration of Puerto Rico, region by region, uncovering the distinct character and highlights of each area.

In San Juan: The Historic Capital, we delve into the city's colonial past, exploring the old city's cobblestone streets, forts, and colorful buildings that tell stories of centuries gone by. San Juan serves as both a window into the past and a bustling modern metropolis with vibrant nightlife, shopping, and dining.

Heading east, you'll discover The East: Rainforests and Beaches, where nature's splendor unfolds in lush tropical rainforests like El Yunque, the only tropical rainforest in the United States National Forest System. This region is also famed for its spectacular beaches that offer tranquil retreats and vibrant aquatic activities.

To the west, The West: Surfing and Sunsets highlights the island's adventurous side with some of the best surfing spots in the Caribbean. Towns like Rincon draw surfers from around the world and treat every visitor to breathtaking sunsets that paint the sky in hues of orange and pink.

The South: Off-the-Beaten-Path Treasures reveals quieter, less explored parts of Puerto Rico. Here, visitors can escape the more tourist-centric areas and enjoy unique local experiences, including boat trips to the bioluminescent bays near Lajas and the cultural richness of Ponce, the island's second-largest city.

Finally, the Central Mountains: Coffee Plantations and Cool Breezes provide a refreshing change of altitude. This region, known for its cooler climate and panoramic views, is home to lush coffee plantations where you can learn about coffee production and taste some of the finest brews directly from the source.

This exploration through Puerto Rico's regions will offer you a comprehensive understanding of the island's geographical and cultural diversity, enhancing your travel experience by connecting you with the essence of each unique area. Whether you are seeking historical insights, natural beauty, adventurous activities, or simply a peaceful retreat, Puerto Rico's regions promise a rich and fulfilling journey.

San Juan: The Historic Capital

San Juan, the capital of Puerto Rico, stands as a vibrant testament to the island's rich history and cultural heritage. Located on the northeastern coast, San Juan is not only the most populous city in Puerto Rico but also one of the most significant colonial cities in the Americas. With its well-preserved historical architecture, bustling streets, and modern amenities, San Juan offers a fascinating blend of the old and the new, making it a must-visit for anyone traveling to the island.

Historic Old San Juan is the heart of the city's colonial past and is a major highlight for visitors. This part of San Juan is famed for its well-preserved Spanish colonial architecture, including massive fortresses, cobblestone streets, and pastel-colored buildings. The most iconic historical sites include El Morro, a massive fort that dates back to the 16th century, and La Fortaleza, the oldest executive mansion in continuous use in the New World. These landmarks not only offer a deep dive into the island's colonial history but also provide stunning views of the coastline.

Getting to San Juan: San Juan is accessible via the Luis Muñoz Marín International Airport, the busiest airport in Puerto Rico and the primary gateway to the island. The airport hosts numerous international and domestic flights, making San Juan easily reachable from almost anywhere in the world. Once you land, the city center is just a short drive away. Travelers can opt for taxis, ride-sharing services, or public transportation to get to their destinations within the city.

For those already on the island, San Juan is connected by a network of major highways making it accessible by car from virtually any part of Puerto Rico. The main routes into the city include PR-1 from the south, PR-2 from the west, and PR-3 from the east. Public buses also run regularly from various towns into the capital.

Navigating San Juan: Exploring San Juan is best done on foot, especially in Old San Juan, where the charm of its narrow streets can be fully appreciated up close. For longer distances within the city or to venture into newer parts such as Condado or Santurce, using public buses, taxis, or ride-sharing apps is recommended. The city also offers a tourist-friendly trolley service in Old San Juan, which is free and provides a convenient way to hop between major sites.

Cultural Experience: San Juan is not only about its historic sites; the city is also a bustling hub of culture, cuisine, and nightlife. From the vibrant streets of La Placita de Santurce, known for its nightlife and culinary scene, to the artistic murals of Santurce, San Juan pulses with the energy of a city that beautifully melds its historical past with a dynamic present. Museums like the Museo de Arte de Puerto Rico and cultural centers such as the Centro de Bellas Artes Luis A. Ferré offer insight into the island's artistic contributions and cultural developments.

San Juan serves as a compelling introduction to Puerto Rico, offering visitors a rich tapestry of experiences that highlight the island's history, culture, and modern-day vibrancy. Whether you are a history buff, art lover, or culinary enthusiast, San Juan provides a fulfilling and engaging experience for all.

The East: Rainforests and Beaches

The eastern region of Puerto Rico is a verdant, natural paradise, known for its breathtaking rainforests and pristine beaches. This area of the island offers a stark contrast to the urban hustle and bustle of the capital, providing a tranquil retreat for nature lovers and outdoor enthusiasts alike.

El Yunque National Forest is undoubtedly the jewel of the East. Located in the Sierra de Luquillo, about 25 miles east of San Juan, El Yunque is the only tropical rainforest in the U.S. National Forest System. As a bastion of biodiversity, it features a dense canopy of foliage, hundreds of miniature ecosystems, waterfalls, rivers, and hiking trails that range from easy walks to challenging treks. The forest is home to over 200 species of trees and plants, as well as wildlife like the rare Puerto Rican parrot and the tiny coquí frog, whose distinctive call is a common sound throughout the area.

Getting to El Yunque is straightforward, with several transportation options available. Visitors can drive from San Juan via PR-3, a journey that typically takes around 45 minutes. Alternatively, numerous tour operators in San Juan offer day trips to El Yunque, which include guided tours and transportation. For those preferring public transport, buses from San Juan can drop passengers close to the rainforest, but a taxi or a hike might be necessary to reach the main entrance.

Just west of the lush confines of El Yunque and before reaching the eastern region, visitors can explore Isla Verde. Nestled in the Carolina area near San Juan, Isla Verde is renowned for its luxurious beachfront hotels, vibrant nightlife, and beautiful sandy beaches. With its close proximity to both the capital and El Yunque, Isla Verde is perfectly positioned for those who wish to enjoy urban conveniences while still being within a short drive of the rainforest. Its beaches offer a variety of water sports and are ideal spots for relaxation after a day of adventure in El Yunque.

Not far from these natural wonders, the northern municipalities of Bayamón, Guaynabo, Caguas, and Trujillo Alto offer a blend of cultural and recreational activities that enrich any visit to the island. These areas, with their proximity to San Juan yet distinct local flavors, showcase Puerto Rico's vibrant suburban life. Bayamón, known for its parks and museums, provides a cultural complement to the natural escapes nearby. Guaynabo, with its fine dining and shopping centers, offers a taste of the island's modern amenities. Caguas invites travelers to experience its rich history and local traditions, while Trujillo Alto serves as a gateway to the scenic lakes and outdoor activities that are less known to typical tourists.

Beyond the lush areas and Isla Verde, the eastern coast of Puerto Rico is lined with some of the island's most beautiful beaches. Luquillo Beach is famous for its golden sands and calm waters, making it ideal for swimming and sunbathing. Just a short drive from El Yunque, combining a trip to the rainforest with a relaxing beach day at Luquillo is a popular option for many visitors.

Further east, the small islands of Vieques and Culebra are accessible via ferry from the town of Fajardo. These islands are renowned for their stunning beaches, such as Flamenco Beach on Culebra, often listed among the top beaches in the world for its wide, horseshoe bay of white sand and turquoise waters. Vieques is also famous for Mosquito Bay, the brightest bioluminescent bay in the world, where visitors can kayak at night to see the waters light up with glowing microorganisms.

Fajardo itself is not only the gateway to these islands but also a destination worth exploring. The town's marina serves as a starting point for catamaran trips to the nearby coral reefs, where snorkeling is a must-do activity to explore the rich marine life.

The East offers a compelling blend of natural wonders—from the dense, leafy paths of El Yunque to the sunlit tranquility of Isla Verde, and the urban diversity of Bayamón, Guaynabo, Caguas, and Trujillo Alto. This region invites visitors to immerse themselves in its natural beauty and urban culture, serving as a perfect example of Puerto Rico's vast ecological, recreational, and cultural diversity. Whether you're hiking through the rainforest, lounging on a sun-soaked beach, exploring suburban museums, or snorkeling in clear blue waters, the eastern region of Puerto Rico offers unforgettable experiences that capture the essence of the island's natural splendor and rich cultural tapestry.

The West: Surfing and Sunsets

The western region of Puerto Rico, known affectionately as "Porta del Sol," is a paradise for surfers and sunset chasers. This part of the island is renowned for its laid-back vibe, stunning beaches, and some of the best surf breaks in the Caribbean. From the legendary waves of Rincón to the serene sunsets over the calm waters of Cabo Rojo, the west coast offers a distinct flavor of Puerto Rican culture and natural beauty.

Rincón, often dubbed the 'Surf Capital of the Caribbean,' is the heart of the surfing scene in Puerto Rico. Located on the island's northwest tip, Rincón hosts several world-class surfing competitions each winter when the Atlantic swells are at their peak. The town's most famous spots include Domes Beach, known for its consistent breaks, and Maria's Beach, where surfers of all levels can catch excellent waves. Surf shops and schools line the coast, offering lessons and gear rentals for both novices and experienced surfers.

Getting to Rincón is relatively straightforward, though it involves a bit of travel from major urban areas. The closest airport is Rafael Hernández Airport in Aguadilla, about a 40-minute drive from Rincón. Visitors can rent a car at the airport, which provides the most flexibility for exploring the region. Alternatively, public buses and taxis are available but can be less reliable and require some planning.

Just south of Rincón, Cabo Rojo offers a contrast with its tranquil beaches and picturesque landscapes. Famous for its dramatic cliffside views and the historic Cabo Rojo Lighthouse, the area is perfect for those looking to enjoy nature and tranquility. The lighthouse, located at the southwestern tip of Puerto Rico, provides panoramic views of the Caribbean Sea and is an ideal spot for watching breathtaking sunsets that paint the sky in shades of orange and pink.

Playa Sucia in Cabo Rojo is another must-visit location for beach lovers. Known for its white sandy beaches and crystal-clear waters, it is a perfect place for swimming, snorkeling, and simply relaxing by the sea. The calm waters here contrast sharply with the rugged surf of Rincón, offering a more laid-back beach experience.

Access to Cabo Rojo is easy via PR-100 from Mayagüez, another major city in the western part of the island. From San Juan, it is approximately a two-hour drive, making it an accessible day trip or a relaxing weekend getaway. The roads are well-maintained, and signs are clearly marked, making it a pleasant drive through some of the island's most scenic areas.

The West of Puerto Rico captivates visitors with its combination of adventurous surf spots and serene beach settings. Whether you're paddling out into the surf at dawn in Rincón or watching the sunset from the cliffs of Cabo Rojo, the western region offers some of the most memorable experiences in Puerto Rico, highlighting the island's natural beauty and its vibrant local culture.

The South: Off-the-Beaten-Path Treasures

Puerto Rico's southern region is a treasure trove of lesser-known gems that invite exploration and offer a deep dive into the island's diverse landscapes and cultural heritage. This part of Puerto Rico, known for its dry forests, serene beaches, and charming towns, provides a stark contrast to the more frequently visited north coast.

Location and Landscape

The southern coast stretches from the city of Ponce, one of Puerto Rico's most important cultural and historical hubs, to the quaint fishing villages of Patillas in the southeast. This area is characterized by its more arid climate compared to the tropical lushness of the north, showcasing a variety of ecosystems from dry coastal plains to rugged mountainous areas.

Getting There

Travelers can access the South via several routes depending on their starting point. From San Juan, the PR-52 highway leads directly to Ponce, making it a straightforward two-hour drive. Along the way, visitors can enjoy the changing scenery, from metropolitan areas to the more subdued countryside. For those coming from the west or east coasts, the PR-2 road connects the southern towns, running parallel to the coast and offering scenic views and easy stops in various towns.

Ponce: A Cultural Beacon

Ponce, often referred to as "La Perla del Sur" (The Pearl of the South), is the region's cultural heartbeat. The city is rich in museums, historical buildings, and art galleries, including the renowned Museo de Arte de Ponce, which houses one of the most important art collections in the Caribbean. The city's architecture, with its neoclassical buildings and charming plazas, tells the story of Puerto Rico's past prosperity and cultural affinity.

Natural Wonders

Beyond Ponce, the south is home to several natural attractions that are off the beaten path but immensely rewarding. The Guánica Dry Forest, a UNESCO-designated biosphere reserve, offers a unique hiking experience through one of the best-preserved subtropical dry forests in the world. Nearby, the beaches of Guánica, like Playa Santa and Gilligan's Island, offer tranquil waters ideal for swimming and snorkeling away from the crowds.

Adding to the southern allure are Guayanilla and Yauco, two towns that encapsulate the region's rustic charm and historical richness. Guayanilla, located along the coast, offers picturesque beaches and a quaint downtown that reflects the area's colonial past. Yauco, known as the "Coffee Town," is nestled in the hills and is famous for its premium coffee plantations. The town's coffee festival attracts enthusiasts eager to taste and learn about Puerto Rico's renowned coffee culture.

Cultural Festivities and Local Cuisine

The southern region is also known for its vibrant festivals and unique culinary offerings, which are deeply influenced by the area's coastal geography. Towns like Guayama and Salinas celebrate seafood festivals that feature local delicacies such as crab, conch, and various fish dishes prepared according to traditional recipes. These festivals are not only a feast for the palate but also provide insight into the community's way of life and their relationship with the sea.

Why Visit

Visiting the south of Puerto Rico offers travelers an opportunity to experience the island's quieter side, where the pace is slower, and the atmosphere is steeped in history and tradition. It's a part of Puerto Rico that contrasts significantly from the tourist-centric locales, providing a deeper understanding of the island's diverse cultural tapestry and natural beauty. Whether you're wandering through the historic streets of Ponce, hiking in the dry forests of Guánica, exploring the coffee culture of Yauco, or relaxing on the secluded beaches along the coast, including those of Guayanilla, the south is sure to provide a memorable and enriching Puerto Rican experience.

Central Mountains: Coffee Plantations and Cool Breezes

The Central Mountains of Puerto Rico, known as "La Cordillera Central," offer a refreshing escape with cooler temperatures and lush landscapes, making it a prime destination for those interested in Puerto Rico's agricultural heritage and natural beauty.

Location and Geography

Spanning the heart of Puerto Rico, the Central Mountains encompass municipalities like Jayuya, Utuado, Ciales, Adjuntas, and extend into Aibonito, Barranquitas, and Comerío. This region's rugged terrain and higher elevations contribute to a cooler climate, ideal for agriculture, especially coffee cultivation.

Getting There

Traveling from San Juan, the journey to the Central Mountains takes approximately 1.5 to 2 hours via PR-52 south to PR-149 or PR-10. These routes provide scenic drives and a vivid contrast as you ascend into the mountains. Due to limited public transport, renting a car is advisable for navigating this less developed area.

Coffee Plantations

The region's cool climate and fertile soil produce some of the world's most aromatic coffee. Haciendas like San Pedro in Jayuya and Buena Vista in Ponce offer tours showcasing the coffee journey from bean to cup, with field walks, harvesting demonstrations, and tasting sessions.

Eco-Tourism and Activities

The Central Mountains are also a hub for eco-tourism. National parks like Toro Negro and Bosque Estatal de Guilarte feature trails leading to waterfalls and rivers, perfect for hiking, bird watching, and nature photography.

Additional Highlights

Adding to the area's charm are the towns of Aibonito, Barranquitas, and Comerío, each with its unique allure. Aibonito, known for its flower festival and stunning mountain vistas, is the highest town in Puerto Rico, offering a cooler climate perfect for nature walks and relaxation. Barranquitas and Comerío, with their rich history and cultural festivals, showcase traditional crafts and offer a glimpse into the island's colonial past through well-preserved architecture and town squares.

Cultural and Historical Significance

The region is steeped in cultural heritage, with Jayuya being a center for indigenous Taíno culture, as highlighted by the Cemi Museum's artifacts. The area's relative isolation has helped preserve many traditional Puerto Rican cultural aspects, from folk music to artisan crafts.

Visiting Puerto Rico's Central Mountains provides a deeply enriching experience that blends natural beauty, cultural depth, and historical insight. Whether exploring coffee haciendas, hiking through pristine landscapes, or immersing in local traditions, this region offers diverse attractions that cater to coffee enthusiasts, nature lovers, and cultural explorers alike.

CHAPTER 8

Attractions and Activities

Puerto Rico, a vibrant island of culture, history, and stunning natural landscapes, offers an array of attractions and activities that appeal to tourists of all interests. From its rich colonial history encapsulated in old forts and plazas to the breathtaking natural beauty of its beaches, caves, and forests, the island provides endless opportunities for exploration and enjoyment. This chapter will guide you through some of the most compelling attractions and activities available to visitors.

Must-Visit Historical Sites in Puerto Rico take you back in time with their storied pasts. The island's history, marked by centuries of colonial rule, is best explored through its preserved architecture and historical landmarks. From the majestic El Morro fort in San Juan to the ancient ceremonial centers of the indigenous Taino people, these sites offer a deep dive into the layers of history that have shaped the island.

Natural Wonders: Beaches, Caves, and Forests in Puerto Rico offer some of the most diverse and spectacular landscapes in the Caribbean. The island's geography boasts pristine beaches, mysterious cave systems, and lush rainforests. Whether it's relaxing on the sun-soaked sands of Flamenco Beach, exploring the mystical caverns of Rio Camuy Cave Park, or trekking through the dense foliage of El Yunque National Forest, the natural beauty of Puerto Rico is both accessible and awe-inspiring.

Museums and Cultural Institutions provide a window into the artistic and cultural expressions of the island. Puerto Rico's rich cultural heritage is showcased in various museums across the island, from the world-class collections of the Museo de Arte de Puerto Rico to the smaller, specialized museums like the Museo de la Música Puertorriqueña. These institutions not only display art and artifacts but also host workshops, performances, and exhibitions that highlight the island's vibrant traditions and contemporary artistic endeavors.

Each of these segments reveals different facets of Puerto Rico's rich tapestry, inviting tourists to not only see but also engage with the island's diverse cultural and natural offerings. Through visits to historical sites, excursions into natural landscapes, and explorations of museums, travelers gain a comprehensive understanding of what makes Puerto Rico a unique and enriching destination. This chapter will provide the necessary information and inspiration to explore these attractions thoroughly, ensuring a fulfilling and memorable visit to the island.

Must-Visit Historical Sites

Puerto Rico is steeped in a rich historical tapestry that spans centuries, marked by indigenous cultures, Spanish colonial rule, and its evolution into a modern U.S. territory. The island is dotted with historical sites that offer invaluable insights into its past and present, making them essential stops for any visitor interested in history and architecture.

El Morro (Castillo San Felipe del Morro) in San Juan is perhaps the most iconic historical site in Puerto Rico. Situated at the northwestern point of Old San Juan, this 16th-century fortress was built by the Spanish to protect against sea invasions. Its massive walls and strategic location overlooking the Atlantic Ocean make it a striking example of military architecture. Visitors can explore the ramparts, dungeons, and living quarters while enjoying panoramic views of the bay and city. El Morro is easily accessible from anywhere in San

Juan via taxi or bus, and it's a pleasant walk from other parts of Old San Juan.

San Cristobal Castle (Castillo San Cristóbal) is another monumental fortification, also located in Old San Juan. It is less than a mile east of El Morro, covering 27 acres—the largest fort the Spanish built in the New World. This fortress was designed to guard against land-based attacks on the city of San Juan, and it features a complex system of tunnels, outposts, and ramparts. Visitors are treated to historical reenactments and can explore the extensive network of tunnels that connect different parts of the fort. San Cristobal is accessible on foot from Old San Juan, and like El Morro, it's a short taxi or bus ride from other parts of the city.

La Fortaleza (The Fortress) is another significant site, serving as the oldest executive mansion in continuous use in the New World. It was originally constructed in the 16th century as a fortress but has been the Governor's Mansion since the 19th century. Located near the San Juan Bay, it's a testament to colonial history and political evolution over centuries. La Fortaleza offers guided tours that must be arranged in advance, providing a deeper understanding of Puerto Rico's governmental history.

Caguana Ceremonial Ball Courts Site (Centro Ceremonial Indígena de Caguana) in Utuado takes visitors further back in time, to the pre-Columbian era. This archaeological site dates back to 1270 AD and is one of the most important indigenous sites in the West Indies. It features several bateyes (ball courts), plazas, and monoliths engraved with petroglyphs. The site is about an hour and a half drive from San Juan, accessible via PR-10. It provides a profound glimpse into the lives of the Taíno people who inhabited the island before Spanish colonization.

Each of these sites provides a unique perspective on Puerto Rico's complex history, from its earliest inhabitants through its colonial period and into its present status. Visiting these places not only enriches one's understanding of Puerto Rico but also offers a tangible connection to the events and people who have shaped this vibrant island. Whether you're wandering the imposing forts of San Juan, stepping back in time at an ancient ceremonial site, or walking the halls of the Governor's mansion, these must-visit historical sites are key to experiencing the true essence of Puerto Rican heritage.

Natural Wonders: Beaches, Caves, and Forests

Puerto Rico is a treasure trove of natural wonders, boasting an array of breathtaking beaches, mysterious caves, and lush forests that invite exploration and offer respite from the bustling city life. Each of these natural features provides a unique way to experience the island's diverse ecosystems and stunning landscapes.

Beaches

Puerto Rico's beaches are renowned worldwide for their stunning beauty, ranging from serene stretches of white sand to energetic surf spots. Flamenco Beach on Culebra is often ranked among the top beaches in the world for its crystal-clear waters and powdery white sands. Accessible by ferry from Fajardo or a short flight from San Juan, it's a must-visit for anyone seeking a paradisiacal beach experience. On the west coast, Rincón is famous for its excellent surfing conditions and spectacular sunsets. This area can be reached by a two-hour drive from San Juan, making it a popular destination for both tourists and locals.

Caves

The island's karst regions house an extensive network of caves that offer a peek into a fascinating underground world. The Rio Camuy Cave Park features one of the largest cave systems in the world. Located in the northwest part of the island, near Arecibo, the park is accessible via PR-129. Tours of the caves allow visitors to see stalagmites, stalactites, and rivers that run through the subterranean passages. Another noteworthy site is the Cueva Ventana, located atop a limestone cliff in Arecibo. A short hike up leads to a window-like opening in the cave that offers dramatic views of the valley below. It's easily accessible from the PR-10 highway, with guided tours available to ensure safety and provide educational insights.

Forests

El Yunque National Forest is the only tropical rainforest in the U.S. National Forest System and a highlight of Puerto Rico's natural offerings. Situated in the northeastern part of the island, El Yunque is home to a vast array of flora and fauna, including rare orchids and exotic birds like the Puerto Rican parrot. The forest features well-marked trails, picnic areas, and towers that offer panoramic views of the surrounding mountains and coast. El Yunque is about a 45-minute drive from San Juan, accessible via PR-3, making it a convenient excursion for nature lovers.

Visiting these natural wonders provides a comprehensive experience of Puerto Rico's environmental diversity. Each location showcases different aspects of the island's natural beauty, from the relaxing beaches where one can unwind and enjoy the sun, sea, and sand, to the adventurous caves that offer a glimpse into the geological past, and the verdant forests that display the richness of tropical biodiversity. Whether you're a beachgoer, an avid hiker, or someone who appreciates the quiet beauty of nature, Puerto Rico's natural landscapes provide ample opportunities for exploration and enjoyment, ensuring that every visitor leaves with lasting memories.

Museums and Cultural Institutions

Puerto Rico boasts a vibrant array of museums and cultural institutions that reflect its rich history, diverse cultures, and artistic achievements. These venues serve as custodians of the island's heritage and are vital in showcasing the vibrant tapestry of its past and present.

Museo de Arte de Puerto Rico (MAPR)

Located in Santurce, a vibrant arts district in San Juan, the Museo de Arte de Puerto Rico is one of the premier art museums in the Caribbean. This museum houses an extensive collection of Puerto Rican art, ranging from colonial religious works to contemporary pieces. The MAPR is not only a hub for visual arts but also offers a variety of educational programs, workshops, and cultural events. It is easily accessible from downtown San Juan via bus or taxi, and for those driving, the museum provides ample parking. This accessibility makes MAPR a key cultural destination for both locals and tourists.

Museo de Arte Contemporáneo (MAC)

Also situated in Santurce, the Museo de Arte Contemporáneo focuses on contemporary art from Puerto Rico and the Caribbean. This museum is known for its engaging exhibitions that often tackle social, political, and cultural issues. Getting to the MAC is straightforward from any part of San Juan with public transport, and it's located just a few blocks from the Museo de Arte de Puerto Rico, making it convenient for visitors to experience both institutions on the same day.

El Museo del Barrio

In the historic city of Ponce, El Museo del Barrio is dedicated to preserving and promoting the African heritage of Puerto Rico. The museum is located in the heart of Ponce, making it accessible by Ponce's public transit or by car from other parts of the island via major highways like PR-52. The museum's exhibits focus on the art, history, and cultural expressions stemming from the

African diaspora, offering a profound look at the multicultural influences that shape Puerto Rico.

Casa Blanca Museum

Located in Old San Juan, Casa Blanca Museum was the first fortification built in San Juan, initially serving as the residence of the Spanish governors. Today, it functions as a museum that showcases 16th-century life in Puerto Rico. Visitors can explore beautifully maintained gardens, historical artifacts, and period rooms that illustrate the colonial era. Old San Juan is easily navigable on foot, and Casa Blanca is a short walk from other historical sites such as El Morro and San Cristobal Castle.

Fundación Luis Muñoz Marín

For those interested in modern political history, the Fundación Luis Muñoz Marín offers an insightful look into the life and times of Puerto Rico's first democratically elected governor. Located in Trujillo Alto, just outside of San Juan, the foundation is set in Muñoz Marín's former home amid sprawling gardens. It features personal memorabilia, documents, and photos that highlight his contributions to Puerto Rican society. The site is best reached by car, and guided tours are available by appointment.

These institutions collectively provide a multi-faceted view of Puerto Rico's societal layers, offering everything from fine art to historical narratives and contemporary cultural explorations. Visiting these museums and cultural centers allows tourists to gain a deeper understanding of the island's identity, celebrate its artistic achievements, and appreciate the resilience and diversity of its people. Whether you are an art lover, history buff, or cultural explorer, Puerto Rico's museums offer enriching experiences that connect visitors with the heart and soul of the island.

CHAPTER 9

Adventure and Sports

Puerto Rico, an island blessed with a spectacular array of natural landscapes, offers a playground for a diverse range of adventure and sports activities. From the depths of its crystal-clear waters to the heights of its lush mountains, the island caters to thrill-seekers and sports enthusiasts alike. This chapter will explore the numerous adventurous opportunities available, highlighting why Puerto Rico is a premier destination for those looking to combine vacation with adventure.

Water Sports

The island's expansive coastline and vibrant marine life make it a haven for water sports enthusiasts. Snorkeling and diving are particularly popular, with the coral reefs off the coast of cities like Fajardo and the small island of Culebra offering some of the best underwater experiences. Here, adventurers can explore a world of colorful coral, tropical fish, and even sunken ships. For those who prefer the thrill of surfing, the western coast, particularly Rincón, provides waves that attract surfers from around the world during the winter months. Whether you're a beginner or an experienced diver or surfer, the clear waters of Puerto Rico provide an ideal setting for these activities.

Land Adventures

Beyond the water, Puerto Rico's rugged terrain is perfect for a variety of land-based adventures. The island's numerous trails lead through tropical forests, such as El Yunque National Forest, offering hikers the chance to immerse themselves in the rich biodiversity of the region. For those seeking more adrenaline, zip-lining through the canopy offers a different perspective and a rush like no other, with facilities like Toro Verde Adventure Park in Orocovis boasting some of the longest zip lines in the world. Each activity is designed to bring you closer to the natural beauty of Puerto Rico while providing an exciting challenge.

Golfing in Paradise

For sports enthusiasts, Puerto Rico also offers world-class golf courses with breathtaking views and challenging designs. Courses like Royal Isabela on the northwest coast provide not just a game of golf but a luxurious experience amidst cliffs overlooking the Atlantic Ocean. Other notable golf resorts include Coco Beach Golf Club in Rio Grande and Palmas del Mar near Humacao, where the lush greens are matched by scenic ocean and mountain backdrops.

Each of these activities presents an opportunity to explore Puerto Rico's diverse environments and make the most of the island's natural assets. Whether you're slicing through the waves, trekking through dense forests, or teeing off with the ocean as your backdrop, Puerto Rico offers an adventure for every interest and skill level. This chapter will guide you through these exhilarating experiences, ensuring you know where to go and what to expect as you embark on your Puerto Rican adventure journey.

Water Sports: Snorkeling, Diving, and Surfing

Puerto Rico is a prime destination for water sports enthusiasts, offering some of the Caribbean's most beautiful and diverse aquatic environments. The island's unique geographical location and coral formations provide excellent conditions for snorkeling, diving, and surfing, making it a year-round haven for underwater and wave-riding adventures.

Snorkeling and Diving

The clear, warm waters of Puerto Rico are home to a vibrant array of marine life and several protected coral reefs, which create perfect conditions for snorkeling and diving. One of the most renowned snorkeling spots is Flamenco Beach on Culebra Island, known for its crystal-clear waters and abundant sea life. Easily accessible by ferry from Fajardo or via a short flight from San Juan, Culebra offers an escape into a world of underwater beauty that is ideal for beginners and seasoned snorkelers alike.

For diving enthusiasts, the island of Vieques, also off the eastern coast of Puerto Rico, provides a more secluded experience with less crowded dive sites featuring shipwrecks, coral walls, and even bioluminescent bays. Dive shops on the island offer guided tours and equipment rental, and it's reachable by ferry or a quick flight from the main island, making it a perfect day trip or a longer stay.

Another exceptional diving location is La Parguera in southwestern Puerto Rico. This area is famous for its diving sites that include coral reefs, mangroves, and the renowned Phosphorescent Bay, where divers can experience the rare phenomenon of bioluminescence. La Parguera is about a two-hour drive from San Juan, with local operators offering boat tours and diving excursions that cater to all skill levels.

Surfing

Puerto Rico's surfing culture is most vibrant along the western coast, particularly in the town of Rincón. Known as the "Surfing Capital of the Caribbean," Rincón hosts several international surfing competitions thanks to its consistent breaks and wave quality. Popular spots like Domes Beach and Maria's Beach attract surfers from around the world. Rincón is approximately a two-and-a-half-hour drive from San Juan, with public transport options limited, making car rental a favorable choice for flexibility and ease of access to various surf spots.

During the winter months, the north coast of Puerto Rico also offers excellent surfing conditions. Isabela and Aguadilla are well-known for their waves, with spots like Jobos Beach and Wilderness Beach providing challenging conditions suitable for experienced surfers. These areas are accessible by car from San Juan in about two hours, and local surf shops provide board rentals and lessons.

These locations not only allow visitors to enjoy exciting water sports but also offer a chance to connect with nature and experience the serene beauty of Puerto Rico's oceanic landscapes. Whether you're floating over a colorful reef in Culebra, diving into the depths near Vieques, or riding the waves in Rincón, the island's waters promise unforgettable adventures that highlight the natural splendor of Puerto Rico.

Land Adventures: Hiking, Zip-lining, and More

Puerto Rico offers a myriad of land-based adventure activities that capitalize on its diverse landscapes, from lush rainforests and rugged mountains to dry forests and coastal plains. For adventurers and nature enthusiasts, the island provides exceptional hiking, zip-lining, and other outdoor activities, each offering a unique way to experience the island's natural beauty.

Puerto Rico's topography offers hikers a variety of trails that range from easy walks to challenging treks. One of the premier hiking destinations is El Yunque National Forest, located in the northeast part of the island. As the only tropical rainforest in the U.S. National Forest System, El Yunque offers well-marked trails that lead to enchanting waterfalls, towering mountains, and panoramic vistas. Trails such as La Mina Falls and Mount Britton are popular among visitors for their breathtaking natural beauty and manageable difficulty. El Yunque is easily accessible from San Juan by car, with a drive taking approximately 45 minutes via PR-3.

Another notable hiking destination is Toro Negro State Forest in central Puerto Rico. This less frequented area offers serene hikes and the chance to enjoy Puerto Rico's lesser-known flora and fauna. The forest features several trails, including an ascent to Cerro de Punta, the island's highest peak. Reaching Toro Negro can involve a more scenic drive through winding mountain roads, typically accessed from PR-149, about an hour and a half from San Juan.

For those seeking thrilling aerial adventures, Puerto Rico does not disappoint. Toro Verde Adventure Park in Orocovis is home to "The Monster," one of the world's longest zip lines. Spanning approximately 1.5 miles, it offers riders an exhilarating flight over the lush canopy of the central mountains. Getting to Toro Verde involves a scenic drive into the heart of the island, accessible via PR-155, which takes about an hour from San Juan. The park offers various zip-lining courses and suspension bridges, making it a must-visit for adrenaline junkies.

Beyond hiking and zip-lining, Puerto Rico's diverse landscapes facilitate a wide range of other activities. Caving is another popular activity, with the Rio Camuy Cave Park offering guided tours of one of the largest cave systems in the world. Located in the northwest near Arecibo, these caves can be reached from San Juan in approximately an hour and a half by car via PR-22. The park provides a unique opportunity to explore spectacular subterranean rooms and underground rivers.

Horseback Riding along the beaches or in the mountains provides another dimension to experiencing Puerto Rico's varied scenery. Notable locations for horseback riding include the coastal areas around Isabela and the hillside trails in Rincon. These activities offer a leisurely yet intimate way to enjoy the natural surroundings.

Each of these activities provides visitors with an immersive experience into Puerto Rico's natural environments. From the heights of El Yunque's peaks to the depths of Camuy's caverns, the island's landscape offers adventures that are as varied as they are exciting. Engaging in these activities not only brings one closer to nature but also offers fresh perspectives on the beauty and ecological diversity of Puerto Rico. Whether you are a seasoned hiker, a thrill-seeking zip-liner, or someone looking to enjoy the outdoors at a gentler pace, Puerto Rico's land adventures promise memorable experiences that resonate long after the journey ends.

Golfing in Paradise: Top Courses

Puerto Rico is a premier destination for golf enthusiasts, featuring some of the most scenic and challenging courses in the Caribbean. Nestled among stunning landscapes, from coastal vistas to mountainous backdrops, these golf courses combine world-class design with breathtaking settings that enhance the playing experience.

Royal Isabela – Located on the northwest coast of Puerto Rico, Royal Isabela is often referred to as the "Pebble Beach of the Caribbean." This links-style course offers dramatic views of the Atlantic Ocean from nearly every hole. Designed by brothers Charlie and Stanley Pasarell, the course is laid out over a series of cliffs, providing challenging play with spectacular vistas. Getting to Royal Isabela from San Juan involves a scenic drive of approximately two hours via PR-22 and PR-2, leading directly to the resort.

TPC Dorado Beach – Situated just a 30-minute drive west of San Juan, TPC Dorado Beach offers a luxury golf experience set in a historic plantation property. This prestigious venue includes multiple courses, but the East Course is particularly famous. Originally designed by Robert Trent Jones Sr. and recently redesigned by his son, it features lush greens, panoramic beachfront views, and challenging water hazards. The resort is easily accessible from San Juan by following PR-165 to Dorado.

Coco Beach Golf Club – Home to the PGA Tour's Puerto Rico Open, Coco Beach Golf Club is located in Rio Grande, about 30 minutes east of San Juan. The club offers two 18-hole courses, both designed by Tom Kite. The courses weave through tropical landscapes, with lakes and bunkers that add complexity and beauty to the game. Travel to Coco Beach Golf Club is straightforward, with well-marked roads from San Juan via PR-3.

Bahia Beach Resort & Golf Club – Also in Rio Grande, this Robert Trent Jones Jr.-designed course is a paradise for golfers. It stretches along the coastline and into the surrounding forest, providing an enjoyable challenge amidst stunning natural beauty. The course is known for its commitment to preserving the natural environment and is certified as a Silver Signature Sanctuary by Audubon International. Bahia Beach can be reached by taking PR-3 north from San Juan.

Palmas del Mar Golf Club – Located on the southeast coast of Puerto Rico in Humacao, Palmas del Mar offers two distinct courses: The Flamboyan Course, designed by Rees Jones, and the Palm Course, designed by Gary Player. Both courses are known for their beauty and challenging play, featuring wide fairways and picturesque views. Palmas del Mar is approximately an hour's drive from San Juan via

PR-30 and PR-53, offering a slightly secluded but accessible golfing experience.

These top golf courses in Puerto Rico not only provide excellent play but also incorporate the island's lush landscapes and ocean views, making each round a memorable experience. Whether you are a serious golfer looking to test your skills on championship courses or a casual player seeking a leisurely round in a beautiful setting, Puerto Rico's golf courses offer something for every golfer.

CHAPTER 10

Cultural Experiences

Puerto Rico offers a rich cultural tapestry that tourists can explore and immerse themselves in through a variety of engaging experiences. This chapter delves into the vibrant cultural scene of the island, inviting you to not only observe but actively participate in the traditions that make Puerto Rican culture so dynamic and unique. From the rhythms of salsa and the steps of traditional dances to the hands-on learning of local crafts and culinary practices, there is a depth of cultural engagement available for every visitor.

Puerto Rico is synonymous with lively music and dance, both integral parts of the local culture. In this section, we explore how music genres like salsa, reggaeton, and bomba are woven into the fabric of daily life and how these forms express the island's history and vibrant spirit. You will learn where to go to see live performances, join dance classes, and even participate in local dance nights where music brings everyone together.

Engaging with Puerto Rican culture can be a hands-on experience through various workshops and classes designed for visitors. Whether it's learning to roll the perfect mofongo, painting in the style of famous Puerto Rican artists, or crafting traditional vejigante masks, these activities provide a direct link to understanding and appreciating the island's artistic and culinary heritage. This section guides you through the best places to learn new skills directly from talented locals.

Festivals are the heartbeat of Puerto Rican culture, showcasing everything from religious traditions to harvest celebrations. This part of the chapter highlights key festivals throughout the year, such as the San Sebastián Street Festival in San Juan or the Ponce Carnival, and offers tips on how to participate, what to expect, and why these events remain so pivotal to Puerto Rican culture.

By integrating into the local cultural scene through music, dance, learning, and celebration, visitors gain a profound appreciation and understanding of what it means to be Puerto Rican. This chapter not only suggests where to go and what to do but also prepares you to dive deep into experiences that will enrich your visit and leave you with lasting memories of Puerto Rico's cultural richness.

Dance and Music: Experience the Local Scene

Dance and music are pivotal elements of Puerto Rican culture, offering visitors a vibrant pathway into the heart and soul of the island. Immersing yourself in the local music scene is not just about listening—it's about experiencing the history, emotions, and community spirit that every beat and dance move encapsulates.

Salsa, the Rhythm of the Island

Salsa music, synonymous with Latino culture, holds a special place in Puerto Rico. The island has produced numerous salsa legends, and this genre remains a staple of the local music scene. For visitors, an evening in San Juan can start at a salsa club like La Factoría in Old San Juan or the Nuyorican Café, where live bands play infectious rhythms that invite even the most hesitant dancer to the floor. These venues offer salsa lessons for beginners several nights a week, making them ideal spots for tourists to learn the basic steps and feel the music firsthand.

Reggaeton and Urban Beats

Beyond salsa, reggaeton, which originated from Puerto Rico, dominates the contemporary music scene. This genre blends hip-hop, reggae, and Latin American music influences, producing an energetic and modern sound that has taken the world by storm. Clubs throughout San Juan pulse with these beats, providing a taste of the local youth culture. A visit to Club Brava, located in the El San Juan Hotel, offers a premium nightclub experience with a mix of reggaeton and international music hits.

Bomba and Plena – Traditional Folk Music

For those interested in a more traditional or historical music experience, Bomba and Plena offer rhythmic insights into the island's African heritage. These genres, often performed live in cultural festivals and by street performers in public plazas, involve drumming, singing, and dancing that are deeply rooted in community storytelling and historical narratives. To experience these musical styles authentically, head to Loiza, a town known for its African-influenced traditions, or catch a live performance at the Centro de Bellas Artes in Santurce.

Learning Through Participation

Many cultural centers and local communities offer workshops where tourists can learn to play traditional instruments like the cuatro (a ten-stringed guitar) or maracas. These workshops not only teach musical skills but also delve into the cultural significance of each instrument. Participating in such workshops or informal jam sessions in local bars can provide deeper insights into the role music plays in Puerto Rican society and its importance in everyday life.

Festivals and Street Performances

No exploration of Puerto Rican music and dance would be complete without attending a festival. From the Fiestas de la Calle San Sebastián in January to the Bomba y Plena Festival in November, these events showcase the best of local talent and offer immersive experiences in music and dance. They also serve as fabulous opportunities to see live performances, where the dynamic interaction between performers and audiences highlights the communal aspect of Puerto Rican music.

Exploring the dance and music scene in Puerto Rico gives visitors an exhilarating way to connect with local traditions and contemporary expressions alike. Whether swaying to the rhythms of salsa, absorbing the beats of reggaeton, or experiencing the communal vibe of Bomba and Plena, the musical landscape of Puerto Rico offers a compelling, joyous, and enriching journey into the island's cultural life.

Workshops and Classes: Learn a New Skill

In Puerto Rico, the opportunity to learn a new skill through workshops and classes is not just an activity; it's a gateway into the heart of the island's culture. These educational experiences allow visitors to delve deeper into traditional crafts, culinary arts, and even the performing arts, providing a hands-on approach to understanding the local way of life.

Puerto Rican cuisine is a tantalizing blend of Spanish, African, Taino, and American influences, making cooking classes a popular activity for visitors. These classes often start with a trip to a local market to select fresh ingredients, followed by a hands-on session where participants learn to make classic dishes such as mofongo, arroz con gandules, or lechón asado. Culinary workshops are not only a chance to learn cooking techniques but also to understand the history and cultural significance behind each dish. Schools like the

Cooking Dance Studio in San Juan or Spoon Food Tours provide such immersive culinary experiences.

Puerto Rico's rich artistic traditions can be explored through workshops in various crafts, including mask-making for the traditional festivals, woodworking, or even pottery. In towns like Loiza, known for its Afro-Puerto Rican culture, travelers can learn to make vejigante masks, which are used during the carnival-like celebrations. Other workshops might involve learning the delicate art of lace-making, known as "mundillo", in Moca. These classes are typically led by local artisans who not only teach the craft but also share personal stories and historical contexts, enriching the learning experience.

For those intrigued by Puerto Rico's musical rhythms, participating in dance and music workshops is a must. Salsa dancing classes are available in many dance schools and some nightclubs in San Juan, offering beginners a chance to learn basic steps and more experienced dancers to refine their skills. Additionally, music workshops may involve learning to play traditional instruments like the cuatro (a small guitar with ten strings), bongos, or maracas. These sessions are often informal, with a focus on fun and participation, making them accessible to all skill levels.

Given the island's diverse ecosystems, some workshops focus on environmental education and conservation practices. These might include coral reef restoration projects where participants can learn about marine biology and help in active reef restoration. Other workshops could involve tree planting or learning about sustainable practices at eco-friendly farms or reserves.

With its stunning landscapes and vibrant street scenes, Puerto Rico is a fantastic location for photography and filmmaking workshops. These classes take advantage of the island's natural light and colorful backdrops, teaching techniques in both digital and film photography, often culminating in a showcase of participants' work. Local photographers and filmmakers lead these workshops, providing insights not only into the technical aspects of the craft but also into the storytelling that captures the essence of Puerto Rican life.

By participating in these workshops and classes, visitors do more than just learn a new skill—they engage directly with Puerto Rican culture, meeting locals and gaining insights that are not typically accessible through more traditional tourist activities. These experiences leave travelers with not only new abilities but also deeper connections to the island and its people.

Festivals: A Guide to Participating

Participating in Puerto Rican festivals offers an exhilarating way to immerse oneself in the island's cultural festivities, where music, dance, food, and traditional rituals come alive in a vibrant display of local pride and joy. Each festival, whether rooted in religious traditions, historical events, or seasonal celebrations, provides a unique insight into the Puerto Rican way of life and its rich heritage. Here's a guide to some of the most notable festivals in Puerto Rico, detailing what to expect and how to fully engage in these dynamic events.

San Sebastián Street Festival (Fiestas de la Calle San Sebastián)

Held in January, the San Sebastián Street Festival marks the end of the Christmas season in Puerto Rico, but it's also a celebration that feels like a new beginning. Located in Old San Juan, this festival fills the streets with artisans, musicians, and dancers. Parades, live music, and craft displays create a festive atmosphere. To fully participate, visitors are encouraged to enjoy the local crafts, taste traditional foods like pasteles and arroz con gandules, and dance to the music from plena bands that roam the cobbled streets.

The Ponce Carnival, one of the oldest in the Western Hemisphere, takes place the week before Ash Wednesday. This event is famous for its vibrant parades, elaborate costumes, and the vejigantes — masked characters that are a symbol of resistance against Moorish invaders in Spanish history. Wearing brightly colored outfits and masks with horns, vejigantes roam the streets playfully scaring people and dancing to bomba music. Joining the dance and interacting with these characters offers a playful and memorable cultural experience.

Each town in Puerto Rico celebrates its patron saint with an annual festival that includes religious processions, fairs, parades, games, and live performances. These festivals vary by town but generally share a common structure that blends Catholic traditions with local culture. Visitors can participate by attending the mass, watching the processions, and enjoying the local food and games set up in the town squares. These festivals are a way to see the deep community ties and the spiritual devotion that characterize Puerto Rican culture.

For those interested in classical music, the Casals Festival, founded by famed cellist Pablo Casals, is held annually in San Juan. This event gathers some of the finest musicians from around the world to perform classical music in tribute to Casals' legacy. Attending concerts and participating in the festival's workshops and talks can be a profound experience for classical music lovers.

A culinary extravaganza that takes place in April, Saborea Puerto Rico is set on the beachfront in

San Juan and celebrates the island's culinary traditions and innovations. Food enthusiasts can participate by sampling dishes from local and international chefs, attending cooking demonstrations, and enjoying the vibrant atmosphere that combines gourmet food tastings with beachside entertainment.

To truly engage with these festivals, it is recommended to learn a few phrases in Spanish as this enhances interaction with locals, who appreciate the effort and often become more open and friendly. Dress comfortably for the weather and the crowd, and be ready to embrace the local customs, whether it's dancing to reggaeton, tasting new dishes, or simply enjoying the lively ambiance that makes Puerto Rican festivals a world-class cultural experience.

CHAPTER 11

Things to Do

Puerto Rico, with its rich history, vibrant culture, and stunning natural beauty, offers a diverse array of activities catering to tourists of all types. Whether you are traveling solo, as a couple, with family, or in a group, the island ensures every visitor experiences the warmth and excitement of its unique charm. This chapter delves into tailored activities that enhance the travel experience for each kind of visitor, ensuring that your time in Puerto Rico is both fulfilling and memorable.

Puerto Rico presents a variety of adventures and experiences that are perfect for the independent explorer. From hiking the lush trails of El Yunque National Forest to exploring the historic streets of Old San Juan, the island offers numerous opportunities for personal discovery and adventure. Solo travelers can immerse themselves in the local culture, cuisine, and music, finding easy camaraderie and community in the welcoming local atmosphere.

Those seeking a romantic getaway will find Puerto Rico's picturesque beaches, secluded islands, and luxurious resorts the perfect backdrop for romance. Couples can enjoy sunset sails, couples' spa treatments, or candlelit dinners on the beach. The island's natural beauty enhances these experiences, making for unforgettable moments of connection and relaxation.

Puerto Rico is wonderfully family-friendly, offering a plethora of attractions that appeal to children and adults alike. From exciting water parks and interactive museums to family-friendly beaches and nature tours, the island ensures that every family member finds something to enjoy. Kid-friendly attractions are not only fun but also educational, making them a perfect blend of learning and entertainment.

Group travelers will find that Puerto Rico caters to a wide range of interests. Whether it's group tours through coffee plantations, snorkeling excursions in crystal-clear waters, or enjoying the vibrant nightlife, there is plenty to keep everyone engaged. The island's variety of activities makes it easy for groups to plan days filled with shared experiences that cater to the tastes of all participants.

Each section of this chapter will provide detailed insights into these activities, helping you plan your visit to Puerto Rico with confidence and excitement. Whether you seek adventure, relaxation, romance, or fun, Puerto Rico's dynamic offerings promise a rich and rewarding holiday experience for everyone.

For Solo Travelers: Adventures and Experiences

Puerto Rico offers a treasure trove of adventures and experiences ideal for solo travelers looking to explore and enjoy memorable moments. With its rich culture, stunning landscapes, and friendly locals, the island provides a safe and inviting environment for those journeying on their own.

One of the quintessential experiences in Puerto Rico is exploring the historic and vibrant Old San Juan. Walking through the blue cobblestone streets lined with pastel-colored houses offers a glimpse into the island's colonial past. Solo travelers can visit the impressive forts of El Morro and San Cristobal, where panoramic views of the Atlantic and detailed exhibits provide a deep dive into Puerto Rico's history. Cafés and small eateries abound, allowing for leisurely breaks to enjoy local cuisine like mofongo or sip on a Puerto Rican coffee.

For those who thrive in nature, El Yunque National Forest provides a lush escape into the only tropical rainforest in the U.S. National Forest System. The well-marked trails lead to enchanting waterfalls and offer spectacular views from the mountain peaks. The forest's rich biodiversity is on full display, from rare orchids to the iconic coquí frog, making it a perfect spot for eco-tourism and photography. Solo hikers can feel at ease as the trails are popular and well-traveled, often fostering camaraderie among fellow hikers.

Puerto Rico's beaches are another highlight, with options ranging from the serene shores of Flamenco Beach in Culebra, accessible via a short ferry ride, to the vibrant surf scene at Rincón on the west coast. Solo travelers can enjoy water sports like snorkeling, diving, or surfing, with shops and schools readily available to provide equipment and lessons. The island's beaches offer not just relaxation and sunbathing opportunities but also a chance to mingle with locals and other tourists in a laid-back setting.

Adventure seekers will find that Puerto Rico does not disappoint. The island's karst region presents unique opportunities for caving, particularly at Rio Camuy Cave Park, one of the largest cave systems in the world. Guided tours reveal impressive underground features like giant sinkholes and subterranean rivers. For a more adrenaline-pumping activity, zip-lining at Toro Verde Adventure Park in Orocovis offers thrilling rides over the forest canopy, including one of the longest zip lines in the world.

Cultural immersion is also a vital part of traveling solo in Puerto Rico. The island's vibrant arts scene can be experienced through its music, dance, and festivals. In Loíza, the traditional Bomba and Plena music provide a rhythmic insight into Puerto Rico's African heritage. Meanwhile, workshops and dance schools in San

Juan invite travelers to learn salsa, enhancing their cultural experience and offering a fun way to engage with the local lifestyle.

For solo travelers, Puerto Rico offers a dynamic blend of history, nature, adventure, and culture. The island's small size makes it easy to navigate, yet its diversity in attractions ensures that every day can offer a new and enriching experience. Whether wandering through colonial cities, hiking in verdant forests, riding the waves, or dancing the night away, solo visitors will find Puerto Rico a deeply satisfying destination that combines the thrill of adventure with the warmth of its people and their culture.

For Couples: Romantic Getaways and Activities

Puerto Rico stands as an idyllic destination for couples seeking a blend of romantic escapades and memorable adventures. The island's lush landscapes, historic charm, and tranquil beaches offer a perfect backdrop for lovebirds to explore and deepen their connection. Whether it's strolling hand-in-hand along colonial streets, watching a sunset from a secluded beach, or indulging in a luxurious spa day, Puerto Rico provides an array of romantic experiences.

One of the most romantic activities for couples is exploring the old city of San Juan. This area, with its vibrant Spanish colonial architecture and historic landmarks, sets the scene for a day filled with discovery and romance. Couples can visit the forts of El Morro and San Cristobal to learn about the island's rich history and enjoy stunning ocean views. The colorful streets of Old San Juan are perfect for leisurely walks, popping into local shops, and trying Puerto Rican delicacies at charming bistros.

For those seeking a more secluded retreat, Vieques Island offers serene beauty and an intimate setting away from the busier main island. Accessible by a short ferry ride, Vieques is known for its pristine beaches, such as Playa Negra, a striking black sand beach that provides a unique and quiet spot for relaxation. The island is also home to one of the world's most vibrant bioluminescent bays, Mosquito Bay, where couples can kayak at night to see the waters glow under the stars—a truly magical experience.

Couples interested in nature and adventure might find a hike in El Yunque National Forest to be a bonding experience. The trails lead through a canopy of greenery to hidden waterfalls and lookout points with breathtaking views. The sounds of the forest, from the chirping coqui frogs to the rustling leaves, create a serene soundtrack to a day of exploration.

For a taste of luxury, several resorts in Puerto Rico offer couples' spa treatments that incorporate local ingredients like coffee, coconut, and rum. These spas often feature private cabanas where couples can enjoy massages to the soothing sound of the ocean waves. Dorado Beach Resort and St. Regis Bahia Beach Resort are notable locations that offer these indulgent experiences.

Culinary experiences also abound in Puerto Rico, providing couples with the chance to savor the rich flavors of the island's cuisine. A romantic dinner can be enjoyed at a waterfront restaurant where fresh seafood is served alongside spectacular views. In San Juan, establishments like Marmalade or 1919 Restaurant are known for their intimate atmospheres and exquisite dishes that make for a perfect romantic evening.

Romantic activities in Puerto Rico are not only about relaxation and quiet moments; they also include adventures that couples can share to make their trip unforgettable. From the calm waters of secluded beaches to the rich history and vibrant nightlife of San Juan, the island offers diverse experiences that cater to all preferences, ensuring every couple leaves with cherished memories of their time together.

For Families: Kid-Friendly Attractions and Fun

Puerto Rico is a family-friendly destination filled with attractions and activities that cater to children and adults alike, making it an ideal location for families seeking a memorable vacation. The island combines beautiful natural settings with rich history and culture in a way that can be both fun and educational for visitors of all ages.

Puerto Rico's beaches are a major draw for families. Many, like Luquillo Beach, are perfect for children due to their shallow waters and golden sands. Here, families can spend the day swimming, building sandcastles, or simply relaxing under the sun. For more adventurous water activities, families can explore the coral reefs through guided snorkeling tours in Fajardo or take a kayak trip to the bioluminescent bays in Vieques or Laguna Grande. These activities provide not only fun but also a chance to teach children about marine life and environmental conservation.

Visiting Old San Juan can be a fascinating trip for families. Walking through the colorful streets and exploring the massive forts of El Morro and San Cristobal allows children to immerse themselves in the world of pirates and colonial history. These well-preserved sites offer interactive tours that are designed to engage young minds, making history come alive in exciting ways.

Puerto Rico has several museums that are designed with children in mind. The Children's Museum in Carolina offers interactive exhibits that cover science, music, and art, providing a hands-on learning experience. Similarly, the Arecibo Observatory, home to one of the world's largest radio telescopes, offers educational programs that introduce families to astronomy and the wonders of the universe.

For families that enjoy nature and adventure, El Yunque National Forest provides a safe and accessible way to explore a tropical rainforest. The forest's visitor center and easier trails, such as the Angelito Trail, are suitable for children, offering them the opportunity to learn about tropical flora and fauna firsthand. Additionally, adventure parks like Toro Verde in Orocovis offer zip-lining and suspension bridges that are thrilling for older children and adults, providing spectacular views of the forest canopy and a day full of excitement.

Cultural experiences also abound in Puerto Rico. Participating in a bomba dance workshop or a traditional mask-making class can be both fun and educational. These activities allow families to immerse themselves in Puerto Rican culture and traditions, offering a deeper understanding of the island's heritage.

Lastly, families can visit the Cabo Rojo Salt Flats and Wildlife Refuge where they can observe a variety of bird species in their natural habitat. The refuge's visitor center provides educational tours that highlight the importance of conservation while giving children the thrill of wildlife spotting.

These family-oriented activities in Puerto Rico offer a variety of ways to learn, explore, and have fun, ensuring that every family member comes away with special memories and a greater appreciation of the island's natural beauty and cultural richness. Whether it's through relaxing days at the beach, educational museum visits, or thrilling adventures in nature, Puerto Rico provides an enriching vacation experience that is sure to delight both children and adults.

For Groups: Activities for Every Interest

Puerto Rico is an ideal destination for group travel, offering a wide array of activities that cater to various interests, from adventure seekers and culture enthusiasts to nature lovers and history buffs. The diversity of experiences ensures that groups can enjoy a memorable trip filled with activities that appeal to everyone.

Adventure and Team-Building Activities

For groups looking for excitement and teamwork, Puerto Rico offers numerous adventure activities. Zip-lining at Toro Verde Adventure Park in Orocovis provides thrilling rides across one of the longest zip lines in the world, perfect for bonding and building team spirit. Similarly, caving in the Rio Camuy Cave Park offers a group adventure through one of the largest cave systems on the planet, allowing exploration of its subterranean waterways and impressive geological formations.

Cultural and Historical Tours

Puerto Rico's rich history can be explored through guided tours of Old San Juan, where groups can learn about the island's colonial past by visiting forts like El Morro and San Cristobal. These tours can be customized to include culinary stops, art galleries, and craft workshops, making them a comprehensive cultural experience. Additionally, the town of Ponce, with its neoclassical architecture and the acclaimed Museo de Arte de Ponce, offers a deeper dive into the island's art and cultural heritage.

Beach and Water Activities

Groups can also enjoy the island's natural beauty through beach outings and water activities. Snorkeling and diving trips to Culebra or Vieques allow exploration of vibrant coral reefs and marine life. For a more relaxed day, a catamaran trip to the pristine waters of Flamenco Beach offers swimming, sunbathing, and on-board dining, providing a perfect setting for leisure and recreation.

Nature Excursions

For those interested in nature and wildlife, guided tours of El Yunque National Forest are ideal. Groups can hike through lush trails to discover waterfalls and panoramic views while learning about the local flora and fauna from expert guides. Bird watching in the Cabo Rojo Salt Flats offers another form of nature exploration, where groups can observe a variety of bird species in their natural habitats.

Culinary Experiences

Puerto Rico's culinary scene provides another layer of group activities. Cooking classes that teach how to prepare traditional Puerto Rican dishes such as mofongo or arroz con gandules offer a hands-on culinary experience that is both fun and educational. Alternatively, rum tasting at a distillery like Casa Bacardí in Cataño gives insights into the history and production of one of the island's most famous exports.

Nightlife and Entertainment

Evenings in Puerto Rico can be spent enjoying the vibrant nightlife. Groups can experience live salsa music and dancing in San Juan's popular bars and clubs, or enjoy a night out at one of the casinos in Condado or Isla Verde. These activities provide not just entertainment but also a taste of the local lifestyle and festive spirit.

Puerto Rico's wide range of activities for groups ensures that every visitor finds something engaging, making their trip both enjoyable and memorable. Whether it's through thrilling adventures, cultural immersions, or relaxing days by the sea, the island offers a dynamic and enriching environment for group travel.

CHAPTER 12

Itinerary

Planning a trip to Puerto Rico can be as exhilarating as the adventure itself, with the island offering a rich tapestry of experiences that cater to any length of stay. Whether you have just a day to spare or can indulge in a more extensive exploration, each moment in Puerto Rico is an opportunity to discover its vibrant culture, breathtaking landscapes, and warm hospitality.

For those looking to capture the essence of Puerto Rico in a short time, day trips designed to showcase the island's highlights are perfect. These expeditions allow you to explore the historical depths of Old San Juan, the lush greenery of El Yunque National Forest, or the radiant sands of Flamenco Beach in Culebra, all within the span of a few hours. Each trip is packed with activities that are not only fun but also deeply immersive, providing a glimpse into the island's diverse attractions.

For visitors with a week to spend, the 7-day exploration itinerary unfolds a more relaxed yet comprehensive experience. This schedule includes visits to the colonial charms of Ponce, adventures in the surf towns of the west coast, and leisurely days soaking in the coastal beauty of the east. The week-long journey balances leisure with exploration, allowing for deeper engagement with each location's unique offerings.

Those fortunate enough to delve into a 2-week deep dive of Puerto Rico have the unique advantage of experiencing the island in-depth. This extended itinerary offers the luxury of time to venture beyond the main attractions into the heart of Puerto Rico's local life. From the coffee plantations in the central mountains to the less-traveled offshore islands like Vieques and Culebra, the two-week guide ensures a thorough exploration of both the beaten paths and hidden gems.

Each itinerary option is designed to ensure that visitors leave with a profound connection to Puerto Rico, enriched by experiences that resonate with their personal travel desires. Whether you're seeking a quick escape, a balanced holiday, or an extensive tour, Puerto Rico's itineraries promise to guide you through a journey filled with beauty, adventure, and unforgettable memories.

Day Trips: Exploring Puerto Rico in a Day

Exploring Puerto Rico in just a day might seem ambitious given the island's rich array of attractions, but with careful planning, you can experience a slice of its beauty and culture. A day trip in Puerto Rico can be an exciting and enriching experience, whether you're soaking in historical sites, natural wonders, or the vibrant local culture. Here's how you can maximize a single day to capture a memorable and diverse Puerto Rican experience.

Morning: Historical Exploration in Old San Juan

Start your day early in Old San Juan, the historic heart of Puerto Rico. This well-preserved colonial district is compact enough to explore on foot, allowing you to immerse yourself in its colorful, cobblestone streets within a few hours. Key landmarks include the majestic El Morro fort, which offers panoramic views of the San Juan

Bay and a deep dive into centuries-old military architecture. Nearby, the smaller but equally fascinating Castillo San Cristobal unfolds its tunnels and bunkers, telling tales of old battles and colonial strategies.

After visiting the forts, stroll through the charming streets to see beautiful Spanish colonial buildings, quaint shops, and vibrant plazas such as Plaza de Armas and Plaza del Quinto Centenario. Enjoy a quick coffee break at a local café, where you can savor Puerto Rican coffee, known for its rich flavor.

Afternoon: Nature Retreat at El Yunque National Forest

Post morning historical explorations, drive to El Yunque National Forest, about an hour east of San Juan. As the only tropical rainforest in the U.S. National Forest System, El Yunque offers a refreshing contrast with its lush foliage, cascading waterfalls, and abundant wildlife. You can choose a trail that matches your interest and fitness level—popular options include the La Mina Falls trail, which leads to a beautiful waterfall perfect for a refreshing swim, or the Yokahú Tower trail, which offers easy access and stunning views over the forest canopy.

While in El Yunque, indulge in the tranquility of the rainforest and listen to the symphony of nature, from the chirping of the coquí frogs to the rustle of the wind through the trees. The visitor center provides insights into the forest's ecosystem and history, enriching your understanding of this natural wonder.

Evening: Relaxation and Sunset at a Coastal Town

To conclude your day, drive to a nearby coastal town such as Luquillo, which is famous for its beautiful beach and kiosks serving delicious local food. Luquillo Beach is ideal for a relaxing stroll along the shore or a dip in the calm waters as the sun begins to set. The beachfront kiosks offer a variety of Puerto Rican street foods, including alcapurrias, empanadillas, and the island's famous pina coladas.

Enjoy your meal and drink as you watch the sunset, reflecting on the day's adventures. This mix of historical exploration, immersion in nature, and relaxation by the sea provides a well-rounded experience of Puerto Rico's diverse offerings, all achievable within a single day's journey.

This day trip itinerary ensures that even travelers with limited time can experience a meaningful and comprehensive glimpse of what makes Puerto Rico a unique and captivating destination.

7-Day Exploration: A Week of Wonders

A 7-day exploration of Puerto Rico offers a wonderful opportunity to dive deeply into the island's rich tapestry of culture, history, nature, and cuisine. This week-long itinerary is structured to showcase the very best of Puerto Rico, providing a comprehensive experience that balances relaxation with adventure and cultural immersion.

Day 1: Arrival and Exploration of Old San Juan

Begin your adventure in the historic heart of Puerto Rico, Old San Juan. Spend your first day wandering through the colorful streets lined with Spanish colonial architecture, visiting iconic sites such as El Morro and Castillo San Cristobal. These massive fortresses offer insights into Puerto Rico's strategic importance during the colonial era. After a day of historical exploration, enjoy dinner at one of Old San Juan's excellent restaurants, where you can try traditional Puerto Rican dishes.

Day 2: Day Trip to El Yunque National Forest

Dedicate your second day to nature by visiting El Yunque National Forest. This tropical rainforest offers a range of hiking trails that lead to picturesque waterfalls and provide stunning vistas of the forest canopy. Popular trails like La Mina Falls or El Yunque Peak are perfect for immersing yourself in the lush, verdant surroundings and possibly spotting some of the island's native wildlife.

Day 3: Adventure in the East – Kayaking and Bioluminescent Bay

Travel to the eastern part of the island to experience the natural wonder of the bioluminescent bays. Spend the afternoon kayaking in the tranquil waters of Laguna Grande in Fajardo. After sunset, you'll see the water come alive with bioluminescent organisms, creating a magical, glowing effect that makes for an unforgettable experience.

Day 4: Cultural Immersion in Ponce

Head to Ponce, known as "La Perla del Sur" (The Pearl of the South), on your fourth day. Explore the city's rich architectural heritage, including the Ponce Cathedral and the historic firehouse, Parque de Bombas. Visit the Museo de Arte de Ponce, which houses an impressive collection of European and Puerto Rican art.

Day 5: Relaxation Day at Flamenco Beach, Culebra

Take a ferry to Culebra, a small island off the east coast of Puerto Rico, known for Flamenco Beach, one of the top beaches in the world. Spend the day relaxing on the white sandy beach and swimming in the crystal-clear blue waters, or snorkeling to explore the rich marine life.

Day 6: Exploration of the Camuy Caves and Arecibo Observatory

Venture to the northwest part of the island to visit the Rio Camuy Cave Park, one of the largest cave systems in the world. Explore the caverns and underground rivers that make up this geological marvel. In the afternoon, visit the nearby Arecibo Observatory, a massive radio telescope and a hub for world-class astronomy research.

Day 7: Leisure and Departure

Spend your last day at leisure in San Juan. Enjoy some last-minute shopping, revisit a favorite spot, or simply relax at one of the city's beautiful beaches. Reflect on the memories made over the past week before your departure.

This 7-day itinerary allows visitors to experience the diversity of Puerto Rico, from its natural beauty and complex history to its vibrant culture and friendly people. Each day brings a new adventure, ensuring that your week in Puerto Rico is not only enjoyable but also a profoundly enriching experience.

2-Week Deep Dive: In-Depth Exploration

Embarking on a two-week deep dive into Puerto Rico allows for an expansive exploration of the island's diverse offerings, from its rich history and stunning natural landscapes to its vibrant cultural scenes and culinary delights. This extended stay affords the luxury to not only visit major attractions but also uncover hidden gems, engage more deeply with local communities, and truly immerse oneself in the Puerto Rican way of life.

Week 1: Comprehensive Exploration of Major Highlights

Day 1-2: San Juan

Begin your journey in Puerto Rico's vibrant capital, San Juan. Spend two days exploring the historic Old San Juan, visiting iconic sites such as Castillo San Felipe del Morro and Castillo San Cristóbal. Delve into the local arts scene by visiting galleries and museums like the Museo de

Arte de Puerto Rico. Enjoy evenings in local salsa clubs or dining at top-rated restaurants offering authentic Puerto Rican cuisine.

Day 3: El Yunque National Forest

Dedicate a day to visit El Yunque National Forest. Take guided hikes to waterfalls and mountaintop views, and learn about the rainforest's ecosystem. Participate in eco-friendly tours which might include bird watching or a night-time walk to experience the nocturnal life of the forest.

Day 4-5: East Coast - Fajardo and Vieques

Travel to Fajardo, known for its clear waters ideal for snorkeling and scuba diving. From Fajardo, take a day trip to Vieques, an island famous for its bioluminescent Mosquito Bay. Spend a night there to experience the glow of bioluminescent organisms up close on a kayak tour.

Day 6-7: South Coast - Ponce

Head to Ponce, the island's second-largest city, known for its rich history and culture. Visit the Ponce Art Museum and explore historic firehouses and plazas. Sample southern Puerto Rico's unique flavors, and if time allows, visit nearby coffee plantations for a tour and tasting.

Week 2: In-depth Exploration of Lesser-Known Areas

Day 8-9: Central Mountains

Venture into the central mountains of Puerto Rico, an area less frequented by tourists. Explore local towns like Ciales and Jayuya, where you can learn about indigenous Taíno culture and visit museums dedicated to the island's pre-Columbian history. Enjoy hiking or horseback riding in the lush settings.

Day 10-11: West Coast - Rincón and Aguadilla

Travel to the west coast, where Rincón attracts surfers from around the globe. Try surfing lessons or simply enjoy the laid-back beach atmosphere. In Aguadilla, explore local beaches and possibly venture into caving or cliff diving, depending on your adventurous spirit.

Day 12: Northwest - Arecibo

In Arecibo, visit the Arecibo Observatory and explore the nearby Rio Camuy Cave Park, one of the largest cave systems in the world. These visits provide a mix of scientific learning and natural exploration.

Day 13-14: Back to San Juan and Departure

Return to San Juan to relax and reflect on your journey. Spend your last days souvenir shopping, revisiting any favorite spots, or exploring any areas of San Juan you may have missed, such as the Santurce district, known for its street art and vibrant market.

This comprehensive two-week itinerary in Puerto Rico allows you to thoroughly experience the island's natural beauty, cultural wealth, and historical depths. Each day provides an opportunity to engage with different aspects of Puerto Rican life, offering a rich tapestry of experiences that will enrich your understanding and appreciation of this vibrant Caribbean island. This immersive approach ensures that your journey will leave you with a deep connection to Puerto Rico and memories that will last a lifetime.

CHAPTER 13

Tips and Tricks for Travelers

Traveling to Puerto Rico offers an exhilarating blend of tropical landscapes, rich history, and vibrant culture. To make the most of your visit, understanding some essential tips and tricks can greatly enhance your experience. This chapter aims to equip you with practical advice that addresses common travel concerns and helps you navigate the island with ease.

First, we'll cover Language Tips: Basic Spanish for Travelers. While English is widely spoken, knowing some basic Spanish phrases will enrich your interactions and show respect for the local culture. This section will provide you with simple, useful Spanish phrases that can help in everyday situations, from ordering food to asking for directions.

Next, we delve into Cultural Etiquette: Do's and Don'ts. Every culture has its nuances, and Puerto Rico is no exception. Understanding the local customs and what is considered polite or rude can go a long way in fostering goodwill and ensuring that your interactions with locals are respectful and pleasant.

Lastly, we offer Budget Tips: How to Save While Traveling. Puerto Rico can be enjoyed on any budget, and this section will give you insider tips on how to stretch your dollar. From finding affordable accommodations and dining options to free or low-cost activities, these tips will help you make the most of your trip without breaking the bank. Armed with this knowledge, you'll be better prepared to navigate the island, interact with locals, and experience the true essence of Puerto Rico. Whether you're a seasoned traveler or visiting for the first time, these insights will help you enjoy a smoother and more enjoyable journey.

Language Tips: Basic Spanish for Travelers

Navigating Puerto Rico as a tourist becomes more engaging and respectful when you can sprinkle your interactions with some basic Spanish. While many Puerto Ricans are bilingual, showing effort in speaking the local language can enhance your experiences, from dining and shopping to asking for directions and expressing courtesies.

Essential Phrases for Everyday Use

1. **Greetings and Politeness**
   - **Hello** - Hola
   - **Good morning** - Buenos días
   - **Good afternoon** - Buenas tardes
   - **Good evening/night** - Buenas noches
   - **Please** - Por favor
   - **Thank you** - Gracias
   - **You're welcome** - De nada
   - **Excuse me/Sorry** - Perdón / Lo siento

These basics help smooth over most daily interactions, showing politeness and respect.

2. At Restaurants and Shops

- **I would like...** - Me gustaría...
- **How much is this?** - ¿Cuánto cuesta esto?
- **The bill, please.** - La cuenta, por favor.
- **Is there a table available?** - ¿Hay una mesa disponible?
- **I am allergic to...** - Soy alérgico/a a...

Being able to communicate at restaurants and stores with simple queries or statements can significantly enhance your shopping and dining experiences, ensuring you get what you need.

3. Directions and Transportation

- **Where is...?** - ¿Dónde está...?
- **How can I get to...?** - ¿Cómo puedo llegar a...?
- **I'm lost.** - Estoy perdido/a.
- **Bus station** - Estación de autobuses

- **Train station** - Estación de tren
- **Airport** - Aeropuerto
- **To the right/left** - A la derecha/izquierda
- **Straight ahead - Todo recto**

Understanding these basics can help you navigate the cities and countryside more effectively, making your travel smoother and more enjoyable.

4. Emergency and Health

- **Help!** - ¡Ayuda!
- **Call the police!** - ¡Llame a la policía!
- **I need a doctor.** - Necesito un médico.
- **Where is the hospital?** - ¿Dónde está el hospital?
- **I feel sick.** - Me siento enfermo/a.

In case of an emergency, knowing these phrases can be crucial for quickly accessing help or explaining your situation to others.

Practice and Usage Tips

- **Practice Makes Perfect:** Before your trip, spend some time practicing these phrases, ideally with a native speaker or through a language learning app. This will help with pronunciation and boost your confidence.

- **Carry a Phrasebook:** Keeping a small Spanish phrasebook or a digital app on your phone can be handy for quick reference in more complex conversations.

- **Be Patient and Willing to Learn:** Locals often appreciate when visitors try to speak their language. Even if you make mistakes, the effort is usually met with encouragement and sometimes, helpful corrections.

By arming yourself with these basic Spanish phrases, you enhance not only your ability to get around but also your overall cultural experience in Puerto Rico. Engaging with locals in their language can open doors to richer interactions and deeper understanding of the vibrant Puerto Rican lifestyle.

Cultural Etiquette: Do's and Don'ts

Understanding and respecting cultural etiquette is crucial when visiting Puerto Rico, as it fosters a sense of mutual respect and allows for a more authentic and enjoyable experience. Here are some essential dos and don'ts to help you navigate social situations, enhancing your interactions with locals and deepening your appreciation of the island's vibrant culture.

Do's

1. **Greet Warmly:** Puerto Ricans are generally very friendly and warm. A polite "Buenos días" (good morning), "Buenas tardes" (good afternoon), or "Buenas noches" (good evening) can go a long way. When meeting someone, a handshake is common, and friends might exchange a light hug or a kiss on the cheek.

2. **Dress Appropriately:** While casual attire is widely accepted, especially in tourist areas and at the beach, it's important to dress more

conservatively when visiting religious sites or more formal settings. Wearing beachwear outside of beach areas is frowned upon.

3. **Be Punctual but Patient:** While you should try to be on time for formal appointments or dining reservations, understand that the local approach to time may be more relaxed. Don't be surprised if events or meetings start a bit later than scheduled.

4. **Tip Generously:** Tipping is customary in Puerto Rico, similar to the mainland United States. Standard tips are 15-20% in restaurants. It's also polite to tip taxi drivers, hotel staff, and tour guides to show appreciation for their service.

5. **Support Local Businesses:** Engaging with and purchasing from local artisans and small businesses not only provides you with a unique souvenir but also supports the local economy. Ask for recommendations on local products or crafts to bring home.

Don'ts

1. **Avoid Sensitive Topics:** Politics, religion, and issues such as statehood versus independence can be very personal and sensitive topics. It's wise to listen more than you speak on these subjects unless you're invited to share your opinions.

2. **Respect Nature and Historical Sites:** When visiting natural parks, beaches, or historical sites, make sure to follow all guidelines, dispose of trash properly, and keep noise to a minimum. Preserving the environment and local heritage is a responsibility that all visitors share.

3. **Do Not Assume Everyone Speaks English:** Although many Puerto Ricans are bilingual, assuming everyone speaks English can be seen as insensitive. It's respectful to ask if someone speaks English before proceeding, and trying to use basic Spanish phrases is appreciated.

4. Don't Take Photos Without Permission: Always ask for permission before taking photos of people, especially in more rural or traditional areas. This shows respect for their privacy and dignity.

5. Avoid Overhaggling: While bargaining is acceptable in certain markets, overly aggressive haggling is not well-received. It's important to be fair and respectful when discussing prices, especially in markets where artisans sell handmade goods.

By following these cultural etiquette tips, you will not only enhance your travel experience in Puerto Rico but also help maintain an atmosphere of respect and appreciation between yourself and the locals you meet. This approach allows for deeper cultural immersion and a genuinely enriching visit.

Budget Tips: How to Save While Traveling

Traveling to Puerto Rico offers an array of experiences from stunning beaches and lush rainforests to vibrant city life and rich cultural heritage. However, like any popular destination, costs can add up. Here are some practical tips to help you save money while still enjoying all that Puerto Rico has to offer.

Accommodation Choices

- **Stay in Guesthouses or Hostels:** For budget travelers, guesthouses, hostels, and budget hotels offer affordable lodging options. These accommodations are not only cheaper than high-end hotels but also often provide a more local experience.

- **Consider Vacation Rentals:** Renting an apartment or house, especially when traveling in a group, can be cost-effective. This option also allows you to save money by cooking some of your meals.

- **Off-peak Travel:** Hotel rates can vary significantly between the high and low tourist seasons. Traveling during the off-peak season can lead to substantial savings on accommodation.

Eating and Drinking

- **Eat Like a Local:** One of the best ways to save on food is to eat where locals do. Roadside food kiosks, known as "kioskos", offer delicious and affordable meals. Local diners, called "comedores", serve hearty portions of Puerto Rican staples at reasonable prices.

- **Cook Your Meals:** If your accommodation has kitchen facilities, consider preparing your own meals. Shop at local markets for fresh produce and try your hand at cooking traditional dishes.

- **Happy Hours and Specials:** Many bars and restaurants offer happy hour specials. Look for places that locals frequent to enjoy discounts on drinks and appetizers.

Transportation

- **Public Transport Over Taxis:** Puerto Rico's public transportation system includes buses, which are a cheaper alternative to taxis. In San Juan, the AMA city buses and the Tren Urbano are both cost-effective and convenient ways to explore the city.

- **Rent Economically:** If renting a car, compare prices between companies and look for special offers. Sometimes, longer rentals can also offer better daily rates.

Sightseeing and Activities

- **Free Attractions:** Puerto Rico has many beautiful beaches, plazas, and historical sites that are free to visit. For example, walking around Old San Juan offers a glimpse into the city's history without any cost.

- **Discounts on Tours:** If you're planning to do paid tours, check for group discounts or bundle deals which often include transportation and meals.

- **Nature for Free:** Natural attractions like El Yunque National Forest are free to enter, though parking might cost. Hiking and beach visits are low-cost ways to enjoy Puerto Rico's natural beauty.

Shopping
- **Avoid Tourist Traps**: Souvenirs in highly touristy areas tend to be overpriced. Shopping at local markets or from street vendors can offer more reasonable prices and the chance to negotiate.
- **Duty-Free**: Consider buying duty-free products, especially if you're looking for branded items, which can be cheaper than at home.

Miscellaneous
- **Travel Insurance:** Investing in travel insurance can save you money in the case of unexpected medical issues or trip cancellations.
- **Mobile Data:** Instead of incurring roaming charges, consider purchasing a local SIM card for

your mobile phone use, which can be more economical for longer stays.

By integrating these budget-conscious strategies, your trip to Puerto Rico can be both memorable and affordable. Being mindful of where and how you spend your money will allow you to enjoy a fuller experience without overspending.

CHAPTER 14

Essential Information

Embarking on a journey to Puerto Rico means stepping into a vibrant world of rich history, stunning landscapes, and dynamic culture. As you plan your adventure, it's essential to arm yourself with key information that will ensure your travels are as enjoyable and hassle-free as possible. This chapter provides you with critical insights and practical tips, serving as your guide to making the most of your visit to this enchanting island.

We begin by exploring the Best Time to Visit: Geography and Climate, helping you understand the seasonal variations and regional weather patterns that might influence your travel plans. Knowing when to visit can greatly enhance your experience, whether you're seeking sunny beach days or wish to avoid the rainy season.

Next, we delve into Free Tourist Attractions. Puerto Rico offers numerous opportunities to explore its beauty without a hefty price tag. From stunning beaches to historic walks through Old San Juan, we highlight how you can enjoy the island's offerings while keeping your budget in check.

Conversely, understanding Paid Tourist Attractions is also crucial. We'll guide you through the must-see paid entries, from world-class museums to historic forts, providing you with options that offer the best value for your money.

Additionally, knowing the Opening Hours for Major Attractions is key to planning your itinerary effectively. This section ensures you won't miss out on what each site has to offer by keeping you informed about when to visit these cultural and historical treasures.

Lastly, for those concerned with inclusivity and safety, our LGBTQ+ Travel Considerations offer insights into the local social climate and resources that cater to LGBTQ+ travelers, ensuring a welcoming experience for everyone.

This chapter aims to prepare you for a seamless travel experience, filled with discovery and delight, by equipping you with the essential information needed to navigate Puerto Rico confidently and comfortably.

Best Time to Visit: Geography and Climate

Choosing the best time to visit Puerto Rico is crucial for planning your trip, as the island's geographical position and climate play significant roles in influencing travel experiences. Puerto Rico enjoys a tropical climate with little seasonal variation in temperatures, which are consistently warm throughout the year. However, there are specific times of the year that might suit different travelers' preferences, depending on whether they are looking for ideal beach weather, wish to avoid the rainy season, or want to participate in local festivals.

Temperature and Seasons

Puerto Rico's climate is generally warm with average temperatures ranging from 70°F (21°C) to 85°F (29°C). The warmest months are typically from June to September, where temperatures can reach higher, making it perfect for beachgoers who want to soak up the sun. Even during the winter months, from December to February, the temperatures are pleasantly warm, which makes Puerto Rico a great winter getaway for those seeking to escape colder climates.

Rainy Season

The rainy season in Puerto Rico runs from April to November, with the peak occurring in August and September. During these months, brief but heavy showers are common in the afternoon, although mornings are often sunny and clear. Travelers during these months will enjoy lush, vibrant scenery, as the rain brings out the rich greens of the forests and landscapes. However, those planning outdoor activities should be prepared for sudden changes in weather and consider packing lightweight rain gear.

Hurricane Season

Hurricane season aligns with the rainy season, extending from June to November, with the highest likelihood of storms typically in August and September. While hurricanes are not a daily threat, it's important to monitor weather reports closely if traveling during this period. Many travelers choose to visit outside of these months to avoid any potential disruptions.

Best Months for Festivals

For those interested in cultural experiences, timing your visit to coincide with local festivals can provide a deeper insight into Puerto Rico's rich traditions. Notable events include the San Sebastián Street Festival in January, the Ponce Carnival in February, and the Casals Festival, a classical music event held in February or March. These months are vibrant and festive, offering visitors a chance to experience Puerto Rico's lively culture and hospitality.

Off-Peak Travel

Traveling during the off-peak months, particularly April, May, and November, can be advantageous. These months typically see fewer tourists, which means less crowded attractions and often reduced rates on accommodations and flights. The weather during these times is usually a mix of sunny days with occasional rain, offering a good balance for those looking to explore both the natural and urban attractions.

Moving forward, understanding Puerto Rico's geographical and climate factors helps tailor your visit to your preferences, whether it's participating in vibrant festivals, enjoying sunny beach days, or exploring the island during quieter, less crowded times. Each season offers unique advantages, and being informed can help ensure that your visit is as enjoyable and fulfilling as possible.

Free Tourist Attractions

Puerto Rico, a treasure trove of natural beauty and cultural heritage, offers an array of free tourist attractions that allow visitors to explore the island's rich history and vibrant landscapes without a hefty price tag. From stunning beaches to historic sites, there are plenty of cost-effective options for travelers looking to maximize their experience.

Beaches

Puerto Rico is renowned for its beautiful beaches, many of which are free and open to the public. Flamenco Beach on Culebra is often listed among the world's top beaches for its spectacular white sands and crystal-clear waters. Similarly, Playa Sun Bay in Vieques offers a picturesque setting with easy access and basic amenities. On the main island, La Poza del Obispo in Arecibo provides a unique beach experience with natural pools formed by ocean waves crashing against rock formations.

Historic Sites

Old San Juan, a UNESCO World Heritage Site, is a must-visit. This historic area is free to wander, allowing visitors to explore its colorful colonial buildings, charming cobblestone streets, and significant sites like El Morro and San Cristóbal forts. While there is a fee to enter the forts, the exterior and surrounding grounds are accessible at no cost, offering breathtaking views and a chance to appreciate the formidable architecture from the outside.

Walking Tours

Free guided walking tours are available in several parts of the island, including Old San Juan. These tours are often led by knowledgeable local guides who share insights into the area's history and culture. Although the tours are free, tipping the guide is customary and appreciated.

Nature Reserves

El Yunque National Forest is one of the few tropical rainforests in the U.S. National Forest System and offers free entry to most of its areas. Hiking through El Yunque provides an opportunity to see waterfalls, lush vegetation, and diverse wildlife. Note that some specific trails or guided tours might have fees, but the general access and most trails are free of charge.

Cultural Events

Puerto Rico has a vibrant cultural scene that includes numerous free events throughout the year. From outdoor concerts and dance performances to art exhibitions and street festivals, these events provide a lively glimpse into the island's artistic and festive traditions. Notable events include the Fiestas de la Calle San Sebastián and the Noche de San Juan celebrations.

City Parks and Public Spaces

Public parks and plazas are scattered throughout the island, offering peaceful retreats where one can enjoy the local vibe without spending money. Noteworthy spots include the Luis Muñoz Rivera Park in San Juan, which faces the Atlantic Ocean and offers ample green space for picnics, jogs, and leisurely walks.

Exploring these free attractions in Puerto Rico not only helps stretch your travel budget but also deepens your connection with the island's natural and cultural offerings. Whether you're soaking up the sun on a pristine beach, delving into the rich history of Old San Juan, or mingling with locals at a festive event, Puerto Rico provides a wealth of experiences that require little more than your curiosity and time.

Paid Tourist Attractions

Puerto Rico offers a rich tapestry of paid attractions that cater to all interests, from historic forts and museums to adventure parks and guided tours of natural reserves. These paid attractions provide structured and often educational experiences that enhance the understanding and enjoyment of the island's diverse offerings.

Historic Forts of Old San Juan

The most iconic paid attractions in Puerto Rico are the historic forts of Old San Juan: Castillo San Felipe del Morro and Castillo San Cristóbal. Managed by the U.S. National Park Service, these forts charge a modest entrance fee. El Morro, built in the 16th century to guard the entrance to San Juan Bay, and San Cristóbal, constructed to protect against land-based attacks, offer a deep dive into the military history of Puerto Rico. Their massive walls, old cannons, and strategic lookout points provide spectacular views of the coastline and a tangible connection to the past.

Museums

Puerto Rico's museums are repositories of the island's cultural, artistic, and scientific heritage. Notable museums include the Museo de Arte de Puerto Rico in Santurce, which features an extensive collection of Puerto Rican art spanning five centuries, and the Museo de Arte Contemporáneo, which focuses on contemporary works from the Caribbean and Latin America. The entrance fees for these museums are typically reasonable and contribute to their mission of preserving and disseminating Puerto Rican culture.

Bioluminescent Bays

Visiting one of Puerto Rico's bioluminescent bays is a magical experience. Mosquito Bay in Vieques, considered the brightest bioluminescent bay in the world, and La Parguera in Lajas, where visitors can kayak or take boat tours after dark, charge for tours. These tours fund conservation efforts and provide educational insight into the delicate ecosystems that create bioluminescence.

Adventure and Nature Parks

For those seeking adrenaline, Puerto Rico offers several adventure parks like Toro Verde in Orocovis, which is home to one of the longest zip lines in the world, "The Monster." Entry fees vary depending on the package chosen but generally offer access to multiple attractions within the park, including zip lines, hanging bridges, and climbing areas.

Caverns and Natural Reserves

The Rio Camuy Cave Park and the Cueva Ventana are two of Puerto Rico's most breathtaking natural wonders, where admission fees contribute to the maintenance and preservation of these natural sites. Guided tours through these caves offer a glimpse into the island's geological history, featuring impressive stalactites, stalagmites, and underground rivers.

Botanical Gardens and Plantations

The Botanical Garden in San Juan provides a lush escape with a small entrance fee, showcasing tropical flora, sculptural art, and thematic gardens. Coffee plantations in the central mountains also offer tours for a fee, providing insight into the coffee-making process from bean to cup, set against the backdrop of verdant hills and cool mountain air.

Investing in these paid attractions not only enriches your travel experience but also supports the local economy and the ongoing efforts to preserve Puerto Rico's cultural and natural heritage. Whether stepping back in time at a historic fort, exploring the luminescent waters of a biobay, or soaring across canyons on a zip line, these experiences form the cornerstone of what makes a visit to Puerto Rico truly unforgettable.

Opening Hours for Major Attractions

Understanding the opening hours of major attractions in Puerto Rico is crucial for planning your visit, ensuring you make the most of your time without facing any unexpected closures. Puerto Rico offers a diverse range of attractions, each with specific operating hours that can vary by season, day of the week, or during holidays. Here's a guide to the opening times of some of the island's most visited sites.

El Yunque National Forest

El Yunque is the only tropical rainforest in the U.S. National Forest System and is open year-round. The forest welcomes visitors from 7:30 AM to 6:00 PM daily. The visitor center has specific hours, usually from 9:00 AM to 5:00 PM, offering exhibits and guided tours that provide insights into the forest's ecology.

San Juan National Historic Site (Includes Castillo San Felipe del Morro and Castillo San Cristóbal)

These historic forts in Old San Juan, significant for their role in defending the island from invasions, are open to the public from 9:00 AM to 6:00 PM daily. During the summer months and major holidays, operating hours can extend in the evening. It's advisable to check their website or contact them directly for any special timings around holiday periods.

Museo de Arte de Puerto Rico

Located in Santurce, this museum showcases an extensive collection of Puerto Rican art. The museum's hours are Tuesday to Saturday from 10:00 AM to 5:00 PM, and Sundays from 11:00 AM to 5:00 PM. The museum is closed on Mondays and major holidays.

Camuy River Cave Park

This park, famous for its large network of natural limestone caves and underground waterways, operates tours from Wednesday to Sunday, from 8:00 AM to 4:00 PM. The ticket office closes at 3:00 PM, or earlier if the daily visitor capacity is reached.

Bioluminescent Bays

The three bioluminescent bays in Puerto Rico (Mosquito Bay in Vieques, Laguna Grande in Fajardo, and La Parguera in Lajas) have varied visiting hours, generally starting at sunset. Organized tours, often beginning around 6:00 PM, are subject to change based on the lunar cycle, as the bioluminescence is best viewed on darker nights.

Arecibo Observatory

Once the world's largest single-aperture telescope, the observatory welcomes visitors from Wednesday to Sunday, 10:00 AM to 3:00 PM. The facility occasionally extends its hours for special events and educational programs.

Ponce Art Museum

This museum in Ponce, known for its extensive collection of European and Puerto Rican art, is open from Wednesday to Monday from 10:00 AM to 5:00 PM. The museum remains closed on Tuesdays.

When planning visits to these attractions, it's a good practice to check the latest information on their official websites or call ahead, as hours can change due to weather conditions, maintenance needs, or special events. Additionally, many cultural institutions and attractions may have free admission days or reduced prices at certain times, which can also influence crowd sizes and visiting hours. Planning with these timings in mind ensures a smooth and enriching travel experience, letting you explore Puerto Rico's rich offerings with ease.

LGBTQ+ Travel Considerations

Traveling as an LGBTQ+ visitor to Puerto Rico can be a rewarding and welcoming experience as the island is known for its inclusive and open-minded attitude. However, as with any destination, it's important to consider some specific aspects to ensure a safe and enjoyable trip. Here's what LGBTQ+ travelers should know when visiting Puerto Rico:

Legal and Social Climate

Puerto Rico is a territory of the United States, and as such, all U.S. federal laws regarding LGBTQ+ rights apply. Same-sex marriage has been legal since 2015, and discrimination based on sexual orientation and gender identity in employment, housing, and public accommodations is prohibited. The island's legal framework generally protects the rights of LGBTQ+ individuals, reflecting a growing acceptance within society.

Community and Culture

Puerto Rico has a vibrant LGBTQ+ community, particularly in the metropolitan area of San Juan. The neighborhood of Santurce is known as a cultural hub with a lively LGBTQ+ scene, hosting many bars, clubs, cafés, and restaurants that are popular with both locals and tourists. The annual Puerto Rico Pride, held in San Juan, is a large and colorful celebration, attracting thousands of visitors. Other events, like the San Juan LGBTQ+ Film Festival, further highlight the inclusive culture of the island.

Safety Considerations

While Puerto Rico is one of the most LGBTQ+ friendly destinations in the Caribbean, discretion can vary depending on the area. Urban areas and tourist spots are generally very accepting, but more conservative attitudes may exist in rural or less touristy parts of the island. As is wise when traveling anywhere, it's a good idea to be aware of your surroundings and adapt your interactions based on the comfort level observed in different settings.

Travel and Accommodation

Many hotels and resorts in Puerto Rico actively welcome LGBTQ+ travelers, with some businesses being members of the International Gay & Lesbian Travel Association (IGLTA). Accommodations throughout the island are not only accommodating but also often participate in LGBTQ+ events and offer packages during Pride celebrations.

Health and Wellness

Access to health services in Puerto Rico is in line with what one might expect in the United States, including support for LGBTQ+ health needs. Several clinics and health professionals are especially inclusive and cater specifically to the LGBTQ+ community, ensuring respectful and competent care.

Local Resources

For LGBTQ+ travelers seeking local community connections or resources, a number of organizations are active on the island. Waves Ahead and Centro Comunitario LGBTT de Puerto Rico are two prominent groups that offer support, advocacy, and recreation activities tailored to the LGBTQ+ community.

Moving forward, Puerto Rico offers a welcoming atmosphere for LGBTQ+ visitors, supported by robust legal protections and a vibrant community presence. Whether exploring the historic streets of Old San Juan, relaxing on the beaches, or participating in local LGBTQ+ events, travelers can find a warm and accepting environment. By staying informed and respectful of local norms, LGBTQ+ visitors can enjoy a rich and fulfilling experience in this beautiful island destination.

CHAPTER 15

Helpful Resources

Embarking on a journey to Puerto Rico presents a wonderful array of experiences, from sun-soaked beaches to rich cultural festivals. To navigate these opportunities smoothly and make the most of your stay, it's vital to have access to a variety of helpful resources. This chapter is designed to equip you with essential information and tips that enhance your travel experience while ensuring safety and convenience.

Firstly, we'll explore the pros and cons of Guided Tours vs. Self-Guided Explorations. This section will help you decide whether to opt for the structured support of a guided tour or the personal freedom of exploring on your own, tailored to your interests and comfort levels.

Next, we address Travel Scams and How to Avoid Them. Here, you'll learn about common pitfalls that travelers might encounter and practical strategies to navigate safely, ensuring that your interactions are as secure as they are enjoyable.

A crucial component of any travel guide, Emergency Contacts and Useful Numbers, will provide you with information needed to reach local authorities, healthcare facilities, and more in case of emergencies. This resource is invaluable in ensuring that help is just a call away if needed.

Health Facilities and Services outlines where and how you can access medical care throughout the island, including pharmacies, hospitals, and clinics, ensuring you stay healthy throughout your travels.

For those planning to drive or use public transport, Transport Timetables and Car Rental offers insights into navigating the island's roads and public transport networks efficiently, along with advice on renting vehicles.

Lastly, Useful Apps and Websites will guide you to digital resources that can simplify travel logistics, from finding the best eating spots to real-time weather updates, enhancing your daily planning and overall travel experience in Puerto Rico.

By arming yourself with these tools and knowledge, you can focus more on enjoying the captivating beauty and vibrant culture of Puerto Rico, while minimizing potential stresses. This chapter serves as your guide to a well-prepared, enjoyable, and safe journey across this enchanting island.

Guided Tours vs. Self-Guided Explorations

When visiting Puerto Rico, travelers have the choice between guided tours and self-guided explorations, each offering unique advantages depending on personal preferences and travel styles. Understanding the differences between these options can greatly enhance your experience on the island.

Guided Tours

Guided tours in Puerto Rico provide structured experiences with a knowledgeable guide who can offer in-depth information about the sites you visit. These tours are particularly valuable for those interested in historical contexts, cultural insights, and local stories that are not readily available from guidebooks or signs.

1. **Expertise and Insight:** Guides often share personal stories and historical data that enrich the visitor experience. For example, a tour guide in

Old San Juan can explain the architectural styles, historical significance, and lesser-known facts about the city's 500-year-old walls and forts.

2. **Convenience:** Guided tours often include transportation, which can be a significant advantage, especially in areas that are difficult to reach via public transport, such as the rainforests or some remote beaches.

3. **Safety:** For adventure activities like hiking in El Yunque National Forest or exploring the Rio Camuy Cave Park, having a guide ensures that you follow safe and environmentally responsible paths, keeping you and the natural habitat protected.

However, guided tours can be more expensive than exploring on your own, and they often have a set itinerary with limited flexibility, which might not suit everyone's preferences.

Self-Guided Explorations

Opting for self-guided explorations gives you the freedom to set your own pace, choose your destinations, and potentially uncover off-the-beaten-path spots that are not included in standard tours.

1. **Flexibility:** You can start your day whenever you prefer, spend as much time as you like at each location, and change your plans on the fly based on your interests or the weather.

2. **Cost-Effectiveness**: Without the fees associated with organized tours, you can often save money, which can then be spent on other experiences like fine dining or unique accommodations.

3. **Personalization**: You have the opportunity to tailor your trip to your exact interests, whether that means spending extra time at a beach, museum, or historical site, or even seeking out

less touristy spots that might not be covered by commercial tours.

The main challenges of self-guided explorations include the need for more thorough planning and the potential for missing out on specialized knowledge that guides can provide. Also, navigating unfamiliar areas can be more challenging and time-consuming on your own.

Choosing the Right Option

The choice between guided and self-guided tours in Puerto Rico should be based on your travel preferences, comfort with navigating new places, budget, and desire for interaction with locals and experts. Many travelers find a mix of both guided and self-guided days offers a balanced approach, allowing for both in-depth learning experiences and personal discoveries.

No matter how you choose to explore, both options open the door to the rich culture, stunning landscapes, and warm hospitality of Puerto Rico, making your trip a memorable adventure.

In addition, here are some reputable guided tour operators in Puerto Rico, offering a range of experiences from historical walks to adventure sports, complete with contact details and indicative pricing.

1. Castillo Tours

- **Services Offered:** Specializes in rainforest tours, historical city tours in Old San Juan, and catamaran snorkeling trips.
- **Location:** San Juan, Puerto Rico
- **Contact:** (787) 791-6195
- **Email:** info@castillotours.com
- **Website:**(http://www.castillotours.com)
- **Price Range:** $45 - $115 depending on the tour type.

2. Spoon Food Tours

- **Services Offered:** Culinary tours that explore Puerto Rican cuisine through the streets of Old San Juan.
- **Location:** 154 Calle Sol #2, San Juan, 00901, Puerto Rico
- **Contact:** (787) 598-6008
- **Email:** info@spoonfoodtours.com
- **Website:**(http://www.spoonfoodtours.com)
- **Price Range:** $79 - $169 per person.

3. EcoQuest Adventures & Tours

- **Services Offered:** Adventure tours including zip-lining, rappelling, and cave explorations.
- **Location:** Road PR-186 Km 45.7, Rio Grande, Puerto Rico 00745
- **Contact:** (787) 889-4015
- **Email:** reservations@ecoquestpr.com
- **Website:** (http://www.ecoquestpr.com)

- **Price Range:** $65 - $135 depending on the activity.

4. Patria Tours

- **Services Offered:** Cultural and historical tours that include visits to significant landmarks and museums across Puerto Rico.
- **Location:** Old San Juan, Puerto Rico
- **Contact:** (787) 545-4545
- **Email:** contact@patriatourspr.com
- **Website:**(http://www.patriatourspr.com)
- **Price Range:** $30 - $100 per person.

5. Acampa Nature Adventures

- **Services Offered:** Eco-tours that focus on sustainable tourism with nature walks, waterfall hikes, and overnight camping.
- **Location:** San Juan, Puerto Rico
- **Contact:** (787) 706-0695
- **Email:** acampapr@gmail.com
- **Website:** (http://www.acampapr.com)

- **Price Range:** $95 - $200 depending on the tour duration and complexity.

These tour operators provide a variety of options that cater to different interests, from leisurely cultural tours to exciting eco-adventures, ensuring visitors can find a guided experience that perfectly matches their expectations for exploring Puerto Rico. Each operator is known for their professionalism and deep knowledge of the local environment and history, making them excellent choices for enhancing your visit.

Travel Scams and how to avoid them

Traveling to Puerto Rico offers a vibrant experience filled with stunning landscapes and rich culture. However, like any popular destination, it can have its share of travel scams that target tourists. Being aware of common scams and knowing how to avoid them can ensure your trip remains enjoyable and stress-free.

Common Scams in Puerto Rico

1. **Taxi Overcharges:** This occurs when taxi drivers take longer routes or inflate rates, especially from the airport or in tourist-heavy areas. To avoid this, always use licensed taxi services and, if possible, agree on the fare before starting your journey. Most reputable taxi drivers use meters, so ensure the meter is running as soon as you board.

2. **Rental Scams:** When booking vacation rentals, tourists might encounter fake listings or misleading property descriptions. Always book

through reputable websites, check reviews carefully, and avoid paying by wire transfer or cash. Using a credit card can offer additional protection against fraud.

3. **Timeshare Scams:** Some visitors might be lured into high-pressure sales presentations with promises of free tours or gifts. These can often lead to misleading contracts for timeshares that are difficult and costly to cancel. If you're not interested in purchasing a timeshare, it's best to decline these offers regardless of the incentives.

4. **Street Vendors and Unsolicited Offers:** You may encounter street vendors selling tours, souvenirs, or other services at seemingly discounted prices. While many are legitimate, some may offer substandard goods or invalid services. Always be cautious of unsolicited offers and purchase from established vendors or stores.

5. Credit Card Skimming and ATM Fraud: Be vigilant when using ATMs and credit cards. Use ATMs in secure locations, such as banks or hotels, and keep an eye on your card during transactions. Cover the keypad when entering your PIN to prevent possible skimming devices from capturing your information.

Tips to Avoid Scams

- **Educate Yourself:** Before you travel, familiarize yourself with common prices for food, accommodations, and transport in Puerto Rico. Knowing the average costs can help you identify when something is unusually high.

- **Use Reliable Sources:** Whether booking a tour, accommodation, or buying any service, use well-known platforms that offer customer protection and secure payment methods.

- **Stay Vigilant:** Always keep an eye on your belongings, especially in crowded places. Carry copies of important documents, and keep originals locked in a safe place.

- **Seek Local Advice:** Hotel staff or local acquaintances can provide valuable advice on avoiding tourist traps and recommend trustworthy services.

- **Report Suspicious Activity:** If you encounter a scam, report it to local authorities or tourist assistance services to help prevent others from falling victim to the same situation.

Being prepared and cautious can help you navigate through common travel scams and allow you to enjoy the beautiful island of Puerto Rico without undue stress. Always trust your instincts—if something feels off, it probably is.

This way, you can focus more on enjoying the vibrant culture, breathtaking nature, and warm hospitality that Puerto Rico has to offer.

Emergency Contacts and Useful Numbers

Having access to a comprehensive list of emergency contacts and useful numbers is crucial when traveling to Puerto Rico. This ensures that you can quickly reach the necessary services in case of an emergency, enhancing safety during your stay. Below is a detailed guide to the key contacts every traveler should have on hand while exploring Puerto Rico.

Emergency Services

- **911:** This is the universal number for all emergencies, including medical, fire, and police assistance. It operates just like it does in the mainland United States, offering immediate dispatch of emergency services to your location.

Medical Emergencies

- **Puerto Rico Medical Emergency Service:** Dial 911 for ambulance services throughout the island. It's vital to know the address or a specific landmark of your location to provide accurate information for a swift response.

- **Hospital Auxilio Mutuo:** Located in San Juan, this is one of the largest hospitals on the island. Contact them at +1 787-758-2000 for emergencies.

- **Centro Médico:** Also in San Juan, this is Puerto Rico's main trauma hospital. They can be reached at +1 787-777-3535.

Police Services

- **Puerto Rico Police Department:** For non-emergency police assistance, call +1 787-343-2020. This line can be used for reporting incidents that aren't life-threatening but require police attention.

Fire Services

- **Puerto Rico Fire Department:** For fire-related emergencies apart from calling 911, you can contact the San Juan Fire Station at +1 787-722-1120 in non-emergency situations for information and preventive advice.

Coast Guard

- **U.S. Coast Guard Sector San Juan:** They can be reached at +1 787-289-2041. Useful for maritime emergencies or to report issues related to water safety and security.

Tourist Assistance

- **Puerto Rico Tourism Company:** For tourist information or non-emergency assistance related to travel and accommodations, contact their line at +1 800-866-7827.

- **CIMEQ911:** This service offers emergency medical coordination (only applies if you have local health insurance) and can be reached at +1 787-754-2550.

Consular Assistance

- **U.S. Consulate in San Juan:** For American citizens needing consular services, the consulate can be contacted at +1 787-522-6200. They assist with lost passports, legal issues, and other emergencies involving U.S. citizens.

Automotive Assistance

- **American Automobile Association (AAA):** For members needing roadside assistance, AAA operates in Puerto Rico. They can be contacted at +1 800-222-4357.

Having these contacts saved on your phone or kept in a handy place during your travels in Puerto

Rico provides a safety net, allowing you to respond effectively to any situation that may arise. Whether it's a health concern, legal matter, or the need for urgent assistance, knowing whom to call ensures peace of mind while you enjoy the rich culture and stunning landscapes of the island.

Health Facilities and Services

Puerto Rico offers a comprehensive range of health facilities and services that cater to both locals and tourists. The healthcare system in Puerto Rico is closely aligned with that of the United States, meaning that travelers can expect high-quality medical care with facilities and professionals that meet rigorous standards.

Healthcare Infrastructure

The island has numerous hospitals and clinics distributed across its cities and larger towns, providing easy access to medical care. These range from large, well-equipped hospitals in metropolitan areas like San Juan, to smaller clinics in more remote regions. Notable facilities include:

- Hospital Auxilio Mutuo in San Juan is one of the largest and most technologically advanced hospitals in the Caribbean. It offers a wide range of specialties and emergency services.

- Centro Médico in San Juan serves as the primary trauma center for Puerto Rico and also houses multiple specialized facilities.
- San Lucas Hospital in Ponce and Mayagüez Medical Center on the west coast of the island also provide comprehensive medical services with emergency departments.

Health Services

In addition to general medical care, Puerto Rico offers specialized services such as cardiology, oncology, pediatrics, orthopedics, and more. Many of the island's physicians are bilingual, speaking both Spanish and English, which is an essential factor for English-speaking tourists seeking medical attention.

Pharmacies

Pharmacies are readily available throughout Puerto Rico, including large chains and independent outlets. Most pharmacies operate within regular shopping hours, with some in larger cities offering 24-hour service. Pharmacists in Puerto Rico are well-qualified and can offer advice on minor ailments and over-the-counter treatments.

Insurance and Payment

While U.S. health insurance is often accepted in Puerto Rico, travelers should verify coverage with their insurance provider before traveling. It's advisable to have travel health insurance that covers medical expenses incurred during the trip, as this can provide additional peace of mind.

Health Advisory for Travelers

Travelers to Puerto Rico should consider routine vaccinations and ensure that they are protected against tropical diseases commonly prevented through immunization, such as Hepatitis A and Typhoid, especially if planning to travel to rural areas or outside typical tourist paths.

Preventive Measures

Given Puerto Rico's tropical climate, travelers should be proactive about health risks related to heat and sun exposure. Staying hydrated, using sun protection, and protecting against mosquito bites (carriers of diseases like Dengue fever and Zika virus) are essential preventive measures.

Moving forward, Puerto Rico's health facilities and services are robust, ensuring that travelers have access to quality medical care. Awareness of available services, understanding local health risks, and preparing for potential health needs can help ensure a safe and healthy visit to this vibrant island.

Transport Timetables and Car Rental

Navigating transportation in Puerto Rico is essential for both maximizing your travel experience and ensuring you can explore the island efficiently. This guide provides detailed information on transport timetables and car rental options in Puerto Rico, helping travelers plan their journeys effectively.

Transport Timetables

Public transportation in Puerto Rico is centered around buses, trains, and ferries

1. **Buses:** The Autoridad Metropolitana de Autobuses (AMA) operates in the metropolitan area of San Juan, providing frequent service within the city and its suburbs. Buses typically run from early morning until late at night, with reduced frequency on weekends and holidays. Timetables can be found at bus stops or on the AMA website.

2. **Tren Urbano:** This is the only rail system in Puerto Rico, serving San Juan, Guaynabo, and Bayamón. It operates from approximately 5:30 AM to 11:30 PM on weekdays and has slightly shorter operating hours on weekends. The trains run every 8 to 16 minutes depending on the time of day.

3. **Ferries:** Ferries operate between Fajardo, Vieques, and Culebra. Timetables for these are crucial as they can change based on weather conditions and demand. It is recommended to check the latest schedule a day before your planned travel, especially if you are heading to the smaller islands for a day trip or longer stay.

Car Rental

Renting a car in Puerto Rico offers the flexibility to explore the island at your own pace and access areas less frequented by public transport:

- **Availability:** Major international rental companies like Enterprise, Hertz, and Avis, as well as local providers, have outlets at the airport and key tourist locations.

- **Requirements:** To rent a car, you typically need to be at least 21 years old, possess a valid driver's license from your home country, and have a credit card. Some companies might charge an additional fee if you are under 25.

- **Driving Tips:** Driving in Puerto Rico is similar to the U.S., with right-hand traffic and similar road signs. However, local driving styles and road conditions can vary, especially in rural areas. It's advisable to have GPS or a reliable map app to navigate.

- **Costs:** Daily rental rates vary depending on the car model and rental duration, with prices starting around $40 per day. Insurance is highly recommended, though your credit card or personal car insurance may cover you in Puerto Rico.

- **Booking:** To ensure the best rates and availability, especially during peak tourist seasons, booking your rental car in advance is advisable.

Understanding and using the available transportation options effectively can greatly enhance your visit to Puerto Rico. With reliable public transport timetables and accessible car rental services, you can explore the diverse attractions of the island, from the vibrant streets of San Juan to the tranquil beaches and lush rainforests that lie beyond. Always plan ahead and stay informed to make the most of your travel time in this enchanting destination.

In addition, here are some recommended car rental agencies in Puerto Rico, including their contact information and pricing details, to help you make an informed choice:

1. Enterprise Rent-A-Car
- **Location:** Multiple locations including Luis Muñoz Marín International Airport, San Juan
- **Contact:** +1 787-253-3722
- **Website:** (https://www.enterprise.com)
- **Price Range:** Starts at approximately $35 per day, with prices varying by car model and rental duration.

2. Charlie Car Rental
- **Location:** Luis Muñoz Marín International Airport, San Juan
- **Contact:** +1 787-728-2418
- Email: reservations@charliecars.com
- **Website:**(https://www.charliecars.com)

- **Price Range:** Approximately $30 to $60 per day, depending on the vehicle and season.

3. Avis Car Rental

- **Location:** Luis Muñoz Marín International Airport, San Juan and other locations
- **Contact:** +1 787-253-5926
- **Website:**(https://www.avis.com)
- **Price Range:** Typically ranges from $40 to $90 per day; rates can vary based on the model and booking period.

4. Hertz

- **Location:** Luis Muñoz Marín International Airport, San Juan and various locations across the island
- **Contact:** +1 787-253-2525
- **Website:**(https://www.hertz.com)

- **Price Range:** Starts from about $45 per day; premium models and SUVs cost more.

5. Sixt Rent a Car

- **Location:** 2036 Calle Celestial, San Juan, 00979, Puerto Rico
- **Contact:** +1 787-791-1991
- **Website:** (https://www.sixt.com)
- **Price Range:** Average daily rates start at $40, with luxury options costing upwards of $100.

These companies provide a range of options from economy to luxury vehicles, allowing travelers to choose according to their budget and needs. Whether you're looking for a compact car for city travel or an SUV for mountain adventures, these reputable rental agencies offer competitive rates and comprehensive services. It's advisable to book in advance, especially during peak tourist seasons, to secure the best rates and ensure availability. Always check what the rental price includes, such as insurance and mileage, to avoid unexpected charges.

Useful Apps and Websites

Navigating Puerto Rico as a tourist is made significantly easier with the help of modern technology. Several apps and websites can enhance your travel experience, offering guidance on everything from dining and accommodation to transportation and local attractions. Here is a guide to some of the most useful apps and websites that you should consider utilizing during your visit to Puerto Rico.

1. Discover Puerto Rico

- **Website:**(https://www.discoverpuertorico. com)
- **Usefulness:** This is the official tourism website of Puerto Rico and serves as a comprehensive resource for travelers looking for information on places to visit, things to do, and events across the island. It offers up-to-date and reliable content that helps you plan your itinerary effectively.

2. Google Maps

- **App Availability:** Available on Android and iOS
- **Usefulness:** Google Maps is invaluable for navigating the island, whether you're driving, walking, or using public transportation. It offers real-time traffic updates, route planning, and the locations of various attractions, restaurants, and hotels.

3. TripAdvisor

- **Website:**(https://www.tripadvisor.com)
- **Usefulness**: This platform provides user-generated reviews of restaurants, accommodations, and attractions. It's an excellent tool for getting a sense of what other travelers recommend and discovering hidden gems throughout Puerto Rico.

4. Uber

- **App Availability:** Available on Android and iOS
- **Usefulness:** Uber operates in major cities like San Juan, providing a convenient and often cheaper alternative to taxis. It's especially useful for visitors who prefer not to rent a car but still want the flexibility of traveling at their own pace.

5. Yelp

 App Availability: Available on Android and iOS
- **Usefulness:** Similar to TripAdvisor, Yelp offers reviews and insights into local businesses, which can be helpful when choosing where to eat or shop. It is particularly useful for finding local dining spots that might not be as prominent on more tourist-centric platforms.

6. PRFerry

- **App Availability:** Available on Android and iOS
- **Usefulness:** For those looking to visit the islands of Vieques or Culebra, PRFerry provides up-to-date ferry schedules and ticket purchasing options, streamlining the process and helping you plan day trips efficiently.

7. Weather Apps (like Weather.com or AccuWeather)

- **App Availability:** Available on Android and iOS
- **Usefulness:** Given Puerto Rico's tropical climate, it's crucial to stay updated on the weather conditions. These apps provide accurate, real-time weather forecasts to help you plan your activities, especially if they involve being outdoors.

8. XE Currency Converter

- **App Availability:** Available on Android and iOS

- **Usefulness:** For international travelers, keeping track of currency conversion rates can help manage expenses. XE Currency offers reliable exchange rate information that can be accessed offline, which is particularly useful for budgeting on the go.

9. Airbnb

- **App Availability:** Available on Android and iOS

- **Website:**(https://www.airbnb.com)

- **Usefulness:** Airbnb offers a wide range of accommodations from private rooms to entire homes, providing a unique and often more personalized lodging experience across Puerto Rico. It's ideal for travelers looking for short or long-term stays with a home-like feel.

10. Booking.com

- **App Availability:** Available on Android and iOS
- **Website:** (https://www.booking.com)
- **Usefulness:** This platform is excellent for comparing prices and amenities of various accommodations. It often features detailed reviews and provides flexible booking policies, which is handy for planning a trip to Puerto Rico.

11. Google Translate

- **App Availability:** Available on Android and iOS
- **Website:** (https://translate.google.com)
- **Usefulness:** This app is incredibly helpful for overcoming language barriers. It supports text translation in multiple languages, including Spanish, which is predominantly spoken in Puerto Rico. The app also has a real-time conversation

mode and can translate signs using the camera on your phone.

Using these apps and websites can significantly enhance your travel experience in Puerto Rico by providing you with all the necessary tools to navigate, explore, and enjoy your stay without hassle. They allow you to access a wealth of information at your fingertips, from planning your daily activities to managing practical aspects of your trip, ensuring that your visit is as smooth and enjoyable as possible.

CONCLUSION

It's clear that this vibrant island, nestled in the Caribbean Sea, offers a richness and variety of experiences that surpass its size. From the historic streets of Old San Juan, alive with Spanish colonial architecture, to the lush rainforests and stunning beaches that define its landscape, Puerto Rico invites travelers to dive into a unique mix of cultures, history, and natural splendor.

Throughout this guide, we've explored the essential aspects of planning and enjoying a visit to Puerto Rico, including detailed insights into the island's attractions, from the famed El Yunque National Forest to secluded spots known only by locals. We've delved into the flavorsome array of Puerto Rican cuisine, a reflection of the island's dynamic history and cultural fusion. Moreover, we've provided practical advice on accommodation, transportation, and navigating the island, ensuring that every traveler can maximize their visit, whether they're in search of luxury, adventure, or cultural immersion.

Tailoring your Puerto Rico experience to match your interests, be it through historical sites, culinary explorations, arts and culture, outdoor activities, or rest and rejuvenation, allows for a deeply personal and unforgettable journey. Engaging with the locals, participating in the island's festivals and traditions, and embracing sustainable travel practices not only enrich your trip but also help preserve Puerto Rico's rich heritage and natural beauty.

Puerto Rico offers a kaleidoscope of experiences, each element a story, a taste, or a memory waiting to be uncovered. This guide is your gateway, an invitation to explore, discover, and fall in love with the allure of Puerto Rico. Whether you're strolling through centuries-old fortifications, swimming in the crystal-clear waters, or enjoying the hospitality of the Puerto Rican people, your journey promises to be an extraordinary adventure. As you turn each page and visit each destination, remember that the true spirit of Puerto Rico is captured not only in its iconic sites but in the spirit of exploration, connection, and appreciation for this gem of the Caribbean.

Made in the USA
Monee, IL
07 December 2024

72030600R00164